JUSTICE V.R. KRISHNA IYER'S CONCEPT OF SOCIAL JUSTICE

JUSTICE V.R. KRISHNA IYER'S CONCEPT OF SOCIAL JUSTICE

VIKRAM SINGH JASWAL
SHWETA JASWAL

DEEP & DEEP PUBLICATIONS PVT. LTD.
F-159, Rajouri Garden, New Delhi - 110 027

JUSTICE V.R. KRISHNA IYER'S
CONCEPT OF SOCIAL JUSTICE

ISBN 978-81-8450-398-2

Typeset by RAHUL COMPOSERS
358, Pocket-B, Phase-2, Sector-16B, Dwarka, New Delhi - 110 075

Printed in India at MAYUR ENTERPRISES
WZ Plot No. 3, Gujjar Market, Tihar Village, New Delhi - 110 018

Published by DEEP & DEEP PUBLICATIONS PVT. LTD.
F-159, Rajouri Garden, New Delhi - 110 027 • Phone : 25435369, 25440916
E-mail : ddpubs@gmail.com • ddpbooks@yahoo.co.in
Showroom :
2/13, Ansari Road, Daryaganj, New Delhi - 110 002 • Telefax : 23245122

Dedicated

To My Father

SHRI JAIMAL SINGH

who gave every help to complete this work

Contents

Preface xi

Abbreviations xiii

1. INTRODUCTION 1
   - 1.1 Concept of Social Justice General Observation 2
   - 1.2 Brief Biography of Justice V.R. Krishna Iyer 4
     - Justice Iyer's Concept of Social Justice 5
     - Social Justice and Justice V.R. Krishna Iyer 8
     - Social and Economic Justice 10
     - Iyer's Concept of Law 12
     - Rule of Law 14
     - His Language and Controversy 14
     - Iyer's View Regarding Constitution of India 15
     - Social Justice and Justice V.R. Krishna Iyer 17

2. HISTORICAL DEVELOPMENT OF THE CONCEPT OF SOCIAL JUSTICE 25
   - 2.1 Ancient Western Thoughts on Concept of Social Justice 29
     - Plato (429-387 B.C.) 29
     - Aristotle (384-322 B.C.) 30
     - Cicero 31

2.2	Religious Thinkers and Concept of Social Justice	31
	Thomas Aquinas (1226-74)	31
2.3	The Classical Era and Concept of Social Justice	32
	Hugo Grotius (1583-1645)	32
	Thomas Hobbes (1588-1679)	33
	Locke (1632-1704)	33
	Rousseau (1712-88)	34
	Benthem (1748-76)	34
2.4	Sociological Thinkers and Social Justice	35
	Roscoe Pound	35
2.5	Economic Thinkers and Concept of Social Justice	35
	Marxian View of Social Justice (1818-83)	35
	Pigou	36
2.6	Hindu Jurisprudence and the Concept of Social Justice	37
2.7	Ancient Indian Thinkers and Concept of Social Justice	38
	Manusmriti and Concept of Social Justice	38
	Kautilya and Social Justice	39
	Ramayana, Mahabharata and Concept of Social Justice	40
	Kabira	41
	Goswami Tulsidas	42
	Guru Nanak Dev (1469 to March 10, 1538)	42
	Saint Ravi Das	43
2.8	Judicial System and Concept of Social Justice	43
	Constitution of Court	43
	Punishment	44
	Islamic Approach to Social Justice	45
	British Era and Concept of Social Justice	48
	Indian Constitutional Development and Socio-Economic Justice	48
	The Round Table Conference	49
	Pandit Nehru's Vision of Social Justice	50
	Gandhian Concept of Social Justice	51

	Dr. B.R. Ambedkar's View on Social Justice	52
	Constitution of India and Concept of Social Justice	53
	The Concept of Fundamental Rights	53
	Directive Principles of State Policy	54
2.9	Planning and Social Justice	54
2.10	Land Reforms and Concept of Social Justice	56
2.11	New Economic Policy and Social Justice	57
	Economic Reforms and their Impact on Poverty	58
	Economic Reforms and Employment	59
	Economic Reforms and Agriculture	59
3.	**DIMENSION OF SOCIAL JUSTICE : IYER'S VIEWS**	**63**
3.1	Classification of Justice according to Justice V.R. Krishna Iyer	66
	Economic Justice	66
	Political Justice	69
	Industrial Justice	70
	Judicial Justice	74
	Distributive Justice	76
	Iyer on Constitutional Justice	77
	Indira Gandhi Asserted	79
3.2	Directive Principles and Social Justice	80
	Organization of Village Self-Government : Article 40	84
3.3	Relationship between Fundamental Rights and Directive Principles	85
3.4	Justice V.R. Krishna Iyer's Views on Relationship between Fundamental Rights and Directive Principles and Concept of Social Justice	91
3.5	Sum Up	94
4.	**JUDICIAL POSTULATES AND KRISHNA IYER'S CONCEPT OF SOCIAL JUSTICE**	**95**
4.1	Justice Iyer and his Judicial View Regarding Social Justice	98

4.2 Justice Iyer's Views on Law and Justice 99
4.3 Iyer's View on Prison Justice 103
4.4 Justice V.R. Krishna Iyer and Reservation Policy 105
4.5 Iyer's Views on Criminal Justice 107
4.6 Iyer's Views on Gender Justice 111
Respected Prime Minister 113
4.7 Sum Up 115

5. CONCLUSION 118

Table of Cases 131

Bibliography 133

Index 140

Preface

The topic of Social Justice has become so important in the contemporary world that almost every government, irrespective of its political and ideological philosophies, places topmost priority to the protection and promotion of social justice in its Agenda of Action plans. But this does not mean to suggest that the idea of human right is of recent origin. On the contrary social justice is as old as human civilization. Social justice is part and parcel of the society.

Justice Iyer's concept of social justice is very dynamic in nature. According to Justice V.R. Krishna Iyer social justice is abolition of various types of discrimination. Justice V.R. Krishna Iyer is champion of social justice. During his judgeship he has given marvelous judgment on the concept of social justice.

Social justice is the ideological signature tune of our Constitution. According to Justice V.R. Krishna Iyer Indian Constitution is a human document.

Iyer's view regarding the Law is but not a machine. Human institution Law and Rule of Law make the society worth living. Law can only make progress in the society when it has human feeling, desire, sentiment and emotions.

According to Justice Iyer Constitution of India is pleasant, but there is need to make the conditioning with socio-economic problem of Indian people. No doubt, it is marvelous socio-economic or human document but needs to be implemented. Therefore in his judgment Justice V.R. Krishna

Iyer tried to implement a Constitutional provision. During his time, Supreme Court of India started to be a Court for Indian people.

My special thanks to Dr. O.P. Chauhan for giving valuable guidelines to write this book. I am also thankful to Dr. Khurshid Alam for valuable help to complete this manuscript. My special thanks to Mr. Rajeev Kumar for valuable guideliness.

The authors wish to express their gratitude to their colleagues and friends, who had frequent meaningful discussions on the subject which ultimately helped them in developing the content of this book. We also express our deep sense of gratitude to the learned authors whose works we have consulted and who have been enlisted in the bibliography. Our special thanks are due to Dr. Sunil Deshta who has been provided his appropriate help and suggestions to complete this work. Our thanks are also due to the various research and academic institutions where from we could collect research material for the purpose of this work. In this connection, our special thanks are due to Incharge, Law Library, Himachal Pradesh University, Shimla and his staff members for their kind co-operation. We also extend our thanks to the staff of general library of Himachal Pradesh University, Shimla, Jawahar Lal Nehru University, Delhi, Indian Law Institute, New Delhi for their help and cooperation. My special thanks are also due to Mr. Naresh Kumar Sharma for his contribution to give the final shape to book. My special thanks due to Dr. Salim and Mr. Rajeev Kumar for help. I am also thankful to Mr. Manmohan Jaswal, Shri Rajesh Kumar, Ahsan Rashid, Piyush Sharma for valuable help. My thanks are due to Shri Roop Singh Thakur (advocate) in H.P. for support. I am also thankful to Pravesh Chandel, Rajiv Rai, Abhishek Lankan Pal.

In conclusion, we would like to put on record our appreciation and deep sense of gratitude to Mr. G.S. Bhatia of Deep & Deep Publications Pvt. Ltd., New Delhi who readily agreed to publish this book.

VIKRAM SINGH JASWAL
SHWETA JASWAL

Abbreviations

AIR	All India Reporter
BC	Before Christ
SCC	Supreme Court Cases
SC	Supreme Court
ILO	International Labour Organization
HR	Human Rights
Cr.L.J.	Criminal Law Journal
JILI	Journal of Indian Law Institute
Lab.IC	Labour Industrial Cases
CMLJ	Civil Military Law Journal
IRDP	Integrated Rural Development Programme
FWP	Food for Work Programme
NREP	National Rural Employment Programme
DPAP	Drought Prone Area Programme

1

Introduction

Today law has become an instrument of social change. Law can prove helpful to bring social change if it satisfies the rules of life. It has human angle and preserve inherent value of life. The distance between law and life is not so long which we cannot see each other. Business of law is life. The concept of man and life demands that law should be equal and provide justice to the society. The history of man is replete with human struggle for justice fair and good conscience. Law is human institution made by human agents to satisfy human wants. Law and life both are co-related to each other. Rule of law should satisfy wants of rule of life. Law is human document and provides the justice to society. The concept of justice is older than that law. Justice is legitimate end of law.

Law and justice both are essential for society. Justice is the end of law. When we talk about law, law should be pro-humanistic approach and should satisfy the human needs and wants. Man is social animal within society and treatment meted to him should be equal, just and fair. Man is sentimental and emotional being and he has emotion and desire. Therefore, nature of law should be according to human. Because man is not for law, but law is for man. Human philosophy requires that law should be according to life. Law cannot be allowed to living coffin of dead soul of justice. The source and course of positive law must be entranced justice. Robert Ingersoll once wrote:

> "We need free bodies and free minds, free labour and free thought, cleanliness hand, fearless brains, free labour will give us wealth, free thought will give us truth."[1]

Therefore, human jurisprudence demands that law should fulfil the grounds of life jurisprudence. It should co-relate with human life, human feelings and human emotions. If law fails to satisfy needs of man, then people will take law in their hands. Law is social institution and has close relation with justice.

Man has been struggling for justice from the very beginning of human society. Justice is an elastic and dynamic concept which varies from people to people, from time to time according to prevailing condition, custom, tradition, religion belief and above all philosophy of life which determines the moral sense of community.[2]

But there are certain norms of justice, equality is pillar of justice. Justice means give every one his due. Today in democratic set-up justice can be divided into following types—social justice, economic justice and political justice. But social justice is the most fascinating terminology in modern social science. Social justice is main features of social institution and in democratic set-up. The concept of social justice thus talks within its sweeps the objectives of removing all inequalities and affording equal opportunities to all citizens in social affairs as well as economic activities.

1.1 CONCEPT OF SOCIAL JUSTICE GENERAL OBSERVATION

'We the people' through representatives assembled in Constituent Assembly adopted and gave themselves to the

1. V.R. Krishna Iyer, Law, Justice and Disabled, (1982), p. 17.
2. Raina, S.M.N., Law, Judge and Justice, (1986), p. 40.

Constitution, tricolour and national anthem—jana, gana, mana symbolize the inauguration of sovereign democratic republic. The Constitution expresses the resolve of the people for building of that 'heaven of freedom'.

> Where the mind is without fear and head is held high
> Where knowledge is free
> Where the world has not been broken up into fragments by narrow domestic wall
> Where the words, comes out from depth of truth
> Where the clear stream of reason has not its way into dreary desert sands of dead habit
> Where the mind is led towards by three into ever widening though and action.

And the world into which Guru Rabindranath Tagore wanted the country to awake, and the Ram Raj which Mahatma Gandhi would wish to be ushered in the country.[3]

The Preamble of the Constitution of India reflects the real mind of the makers of Constitution. The Constitution law is the highest law of the land. Constitution of India is based on the concept of social, economic and political justice. The concept of social justice has been enshrined in Part II and IV of the Constitution of India which show the inclination of Constitution-makers towards socialistic pattern of State. Articles 37, 38, 39, 40, 41, 42, 43 to 51 talks about social, economic justice. These provisions of the Constitution of India are product of matured and socially cultivated mind. The content of social justice was best expressed by Nehru.

> The service of India means the service of millions who suffers. It means the ending of poverty and ignorance and disease and inequality of opportunity. The ambition of great man our generation has been wipes the tear from every eye. That may be beyond use but as long as there are tears and suffering our work will not over.[4]

3. Kagzi, M.C., The Constitution of India, (2004), p. 946.
4. Prabhu Chawla, Equality and Justice in East and West, (1980), p. 27.

The aim of Constitution is not only to provide certain liberties but want to actualization of these liberties to the common man of society. Therefore, in Constitution of India social justice has pride place with various provisions of social welfare of the society.

1.2 BRIEF BIOGRAPHY OF JUSTICE V.R. KRISHNA IYER

Before evaluating the concept of social justice of Iyer, we should scrutinize his life. Therefore, we shall draw some lines on justice Krishna Iyer.

Justice Vaidyanathpram Rama Ayar Krishna Iyer was born on November 15, 1915 at Palaghat in Kerala State. His father was a prosperous lawyer in small sea side town of Tellicherry, Kerala. Justice Iyer took his degree in law from Madras University. He started his practice in 1938 under his father. Mr. Krishna Iyer kept upto crusade for agrarian and labour reform as legislator in the Kerala Assembly from 1952 to 1956 as Law Minster in the first communist ministry under Mr. E.M.S. Namboodripad in his native state.

Resuming legal practice in 1959 Justice Krishna Iyer joined the bench nine year later as judge in Kerala High Court. He became Justice of Supreme Court of India in 1973. Justice V.R. Krishna Iyer is man of conventional sense and had deep approach of humanism. Justice Krishna Iyer is phenomenon, and one man army against injustice and as indefeasible, upholder of all just cause. Many Indian researchers and thinkers have examined different aspects of Indian Constitution from time to time. But contribution of Justice V.R. Krishna Iyer is greater and remarkable one. Justice Iyer has deep passion for downtrodden people. He is man of conventional sense. For him social justice is signature tune of the Constitution of India. But main subject of Constitution is the concept of man. Due to his contribution various Universities of India has conferred him with three Doctorates. He is author of sixty books and many articles. The President of India has conferred on him Padam Bhushan. The President of Russia has conferred on him 'The Order of Friendship' the highest civilian award for foreigner.

Justice Iyer's Concept of Social Justice

Justice Iyer's concept of social justice is very dynamic in nature. According to Justice Krishna Iyer social justice is abolition of various types of discriminations. Justice V.R. Krishna Iyer is Champion of social justice. During his judgeship he has given marvelous judgments on the concept of social justice.

Social justice, the ideological signature of our Constitution is vasundhara katumbkam or lokah samastha sakno bhavantu which is finger print of our cultural heritage.[5] It has already been successfully evolved and adopted in the Constitution of India sovereign, socialistic and democratic Republic which has been given by them. Concept of Justice Iyer regarding social justice is based on the concept of economic justice. He always said that law is satellite of economic structure. He always gave stress on the implementation of directive principles of the state policy.

> "Justice without power is inefficient, power without justice is tyranny. Justice without power is opposed, because there are always wicked men. Power without justice is soon questioned. Justice and power must, therefore, be brought together, so whatever is just may be powerful and whatever is powerful may be just."
>
> —*Blaise Pascal*[6]

Human life is inconceivable not only without maternal production. It is also inconceivable without intellectual production, without social consciousness. People are endowed with remarkable natural gift-consciousness, the ability to feel and think. Social consciousness is the consciousness of people living in society. Consciousness is from the very beginning of social product, and remains so long as man exists at all.[7] Justice V.R. Krishna Iyer is conscious and passionate about social justice. Concept of Justice Iyer about justice is very much clear and strongly supported abolition of all social, political

---

5. V.R. Krishna Iyer, Law *versus* Justice, (1981), p. 51.
6. Quoted in V.R. Krishna Iyer, Law *v.* Justice, 1981, p. 174.
7. V.D. Zotor, The Marxist Leninist Theory of Society, (1985), p. 232.

and economic discrimination. Justice Krishna Iyer is a phenomenon, a one man army against injustice and an indefatigable upholder of all just cause.[8] His mission in life can be summed up in the morning poem of Emily Dickinson:

> If I can stop one heart from braking
> I shall not live in vain
> If I can ease one life the aching or cool one pain
> Or help on fainting robin unto its nest again
> I shall not live in vain

Justice Krishna Iyer has not lived in vain. He is man of austere conventional sense. He fully supported general public cause. He is modest, cultivated man in his functioning and justice delivery system. Being a socialistic he always supported social, economic and political justice. The Constitution of India has created a socialistic republic and in several places repeats the social justice including the right to life in its widest amplitude and the right to an adequate means to livelihood plus opportunities and facilities for children development in healthy manner and in condition of freedom and dignity and interdiction of moral and material abandonment.[9]

Social justice is baloney if appalling condition grip large chunks of political double speak of ruling elite. The villages are without essential needs for landless tillers, feudal greed holding onto hand and other resources, with the state supporting haves while passing colour wash legislation on land reform and urban land ceiling. Such laws hang limp and no single acre has been given to poor. The right to housing is thus dead letter. The rhetoric of Constitution sounds hollow.[10] Justice Iyer always advocated for implementation of directive principles. In the treasury of his sixty books he always quoted Articles 38 and 39 of the directive principles of state policy. State to secure a social order for promotion of welfare of the people.

---

8. M.P.R. Nair, Justice Krishna Iyer at 90, (2005), p. 21.
9. Justice V.R. Krishna Iyer, Human Rights—A Judge Miscellany, (1995), pp. 73-74.
10. *Id.*, at p. 73.

The State shall strive to promote the welfare of the people by securing and protecting as effectively as it may a social order in which justice, social, economic and political, shall inform all the institutions of the national life.

Article 39—Certain principles of policy to be followed by state.

The State shall, in particular, direct its policy towards securing :

(a) That the citizens, men and women equally, have the right to an adequate means of livelihood;
(b) That the ownership and control of the material resources of the community are so distributed as best to sub-serve the common good;
(c) That the operation of the economic system does not result in the concentration of wealth and means of production to the common detriment;
(d) That there is equal pay for equal work for both men and women;
(e) That the health and strength of workers, men and women, and the tender age of children are not abused and that citizens are not forced by economic necessity to enter avocations unsuited to their age or strength;[11] and
(f) That child are given opportunities and facilities to develop in a healthy manner and in conditions of freedom and dignity and that childhood and youth are protected against exploitation and against moral and material abandonment.

In this way Justice V.R. Krishna Iyer strongly supported for implementation of directive principles. In his various judgments he supported that fundamental rights should be interpreted in the light of directive principles. Constitution of India is a social document as said by Austin which contains 98,000 words and 108 words of preamble and moreover major portion of the Constitution deals with concept of social justice.

11. Justice V.R. Krishna Iyer, Social Justice—Sunset or Dawn, (1993), p. 52.

The Constitution, in its preamble and fundamental rights part has inscribed the right to use with equality and social justice to every person who is member of the grand collective, we the people of India as a guaranteed right and paramount value.[12] The concept of social justice of V.R. Krishna Iyer is very vivid and dynamic one.

Social Justice and Justice V.R. Krishna Iyer

Ever since the birth of society justice has been one of the most important quests of human endeavor. Justice means give the one what is due to him. As a principle of law justice delimits and harmonies the conflict desires, claim and interest in social life of the people.[13]

Today the republic is constitutionally socialist. From here we may glimpse the concept of social justice as articulated in the Article of our legal bible, the Constitution, which binds judge and lawyer, government and opposition, management and workers.[14]

Constitution of India talks about social, political and economic justice. The preamble of the Constitution of India starts with the words 'we the people of India' which clear-cut indicates the social interest of common man. Iyer concept of social justice is very clear that he wants to abolish all types of discrimination against human beings living within the society. In socialistic pattern of society, the means of production and distribution in the hands of common man. In that structure social justice is important part of that system. We cannot ignore the social justice while we talk about socialistic, democratic society.

The central theme of this chapter is a blend of jurisprudence and social science with topical reflections. Social justice in the setting of our massive, materials, misery, the product of social injustice, inherited and augmented, before and after independence.[15]

12. Justice V.R. Krishna Iyer, Judge's Postpouri, (2007), p. 15.
13. Sudesh Kumar Sharma, Distributive Justice under Indian Constitution, (1989), p. 9.
14. Justice V.R. Krishna Iyer, A Random Miscellany, Legal and Other, (1984), p. 8.
15. Justice V.R. Krishna Iyer, Indian Social Justice in Crisis, (1983), p. 7.

Our whole freedom struggle for social justice and social democracy is based on the principle that man is a social beings, he wants justice, freedom and equality. Society is not sum of people. Man has various dimensions whether it may be social, moral, cultural, economic, etc. The problem of man cannot be solved without knowing the relationship between man and society. A person's whole intellectual make-up bears the clear imprint of the life of society as a whole. All his practical activities are individual expression of the historically formed social practice of humanity. Man can develop himself when he gets fair means of development. Justice Iyer is of the opinion that man's development is based on the society. Therefore, in his books he says that we have the same Constitution like America but out interpretation comes differently from American jurisprudence, basic reason is that our social and economic condition is different from American jurisprudence and economic development.

Justice Krishna Iyer in his book 'Social Justice—Sunset and Dawn' gave a comprehensive sense. "The concept of social justice thus takes within its sweep the objective of removing all inequalities and affording opportunities to all citizens in social affairs as well as economic activities."

Iyer's concept of social justice demands exploitation-less society by man to man. Social justice, the ideological signature of our Constitution, vasundhra kutumbkam or lokah somusthu sukhino bhavantu which is the finger print of cultural heritage.[16] Law cannot got it alone and its functional competence as the man delivery system of social justice involves the manage with administration know how and collaboration of the agencies in sister department.[17] Main function of law is to make balance between different interests of society. The ultimate guardian of law is not policeman or judge, but the public opinion, informed by the new value system and aware of perils of constitutional disorder.[18] Justice Iyer quoted these lines:

16. Justice V.R. Krishna Iyer, *op. cit.*, p. 38.
17. *Id.*, p. 25.
18. Justice V.R. Krishna Iyer, Social Mission of Law, (1971), p. 62.

> "The law locks up both man and women who steals the goose from off the common. But, lets the greater felon loose who steals the common from the goose".[19]

Justice Krishna Iyer believes that the individual for example is not alone traveller amid the jungle of existence. He is part of world interacting in various ways with the world. Iyer says that whole development of man is based on social existence. If our societies give just system in other words each according to his needs and each according to necessity then no problematic incident can occur in society and crime rate will decrease. Man is not physical equipment but emotional and sentimental living organism. He wants just order, equality and freedom of speech. Social justice means that when man live within society, he must be awarded with just fair means. Justice Iyer talks about common man's justice and his urge for social justice. He is austere phenomenon of social justice during his judgeship in the Supreme Court of India. His strong passion towards humanism makes him one of the best judges in judicial history of India. He regarded law as an instrument of social engineering, as powerful tools in the hands of society for the purpose of reaching social justice to the common man.[20] He always held the little India in his mind and whatever he did or said judicially or extra judicially was directly solely towards improving the living conditions of large masses of people in the country suffering from want and destitution. He always believed that law cannot afford to remain brooding omnipotence in the sky but it must come down the earth.[21]

Social and Economic Justice

Justice Iyer demanded that there should be common ownership of the means of production and distribution. Because economy is the base of all social life and social development. Social justice has also come out from economic structure and development. On the other hand, social justice is

19. Justice V.R. Krishna Iyer, Law *v.* Justice, (1981), p. 11.
20. M.P.R. Nair, Justice Krishna Iyer, (2007), p. 26.
21. *Id.*, pp. 26-27.

the signature tune of our Constitution and little man in peril of losing his liberty in the consumer of social justice. A nobler sentiment than this is hard to find.[22] Iyer demanded that there should be practical implementation of the Constitution of India. Iyer's analysis regarding social justice is based on the non-discrimination. When our Constitution talks about equality and equal opportunity in all fields, then there is need for actualization of Constitution of India. The Principle aim of socialistic state is to eliminate inequality in income and status and standard of life. The basic framework of socialism is to provide a decent standard of life to the working people and especially provide security term cradle to grave. This amongst other on economic side envisages economic equality and equitable distribution of income.[23] Economic equality can bring social justice to the society.

The Constitution of India has creates socialistic republic and several places repeats the right to social justice, including the right to life in its widest amplitude and the right to an adequate means of livehihood. If we fail to provide adequate means of livelihood in that scenario our Constitution has no relevancy. Social justice deals with common man's problem. Therefore, Justice Iyer quoted lines of Pandit Jawahar Lal Nehru in his book legally speaking—

> Our final aim can only be classless society with equal economic justice and opportunity to all, a society organized on planned basis for the raising making to higher material and culture level. Everything that comes in the way will have to be removed, gently if possible, forcibly if necessary. And there seems to be little doubt that coercion will often necessary.[24]

In brief it can be said that Justice Iyer concept of social justice deals with economic justice. If economic justice is possible only then we assume the social justice in society. For acquition of economic justice there is essence of common

22. *Id.*, at p. 89.
23. V.R. Krishna Iyer, Human Rights—A Judge Miscellany, (1995), p. 35.
24. V.R. Krishna Iyer, Legally Speaking, (2003), p. 167.

ownership of the industry than we can assume social justice in Indian society. Economy is the base of all social life. Society is neither a simple nor an intricate sum of people. Individual is not isolated inhabitant of globe. He is social being. In order to live and enforce people to enter into diverse relation and link with each other production, political, judicial, moral, religious and many other. Iyer is of the opinion that if any body access the society first of all he has to study economic condition of that society. Frankly it can be said that—

> Law can never be higher than economic order, cultural development of society brought to pass by that economic order.[25]

Therefore, Iyer is in favour of socialistic pattern of state than only can social justice be possible in that pattern. Iyer quoted lines of U.S. President—

> Every gun that is made, every warship launched, every rocket fired signifies in the final sense a theft from those who hunger and are not fed, those who are cold and are not clothed. This world in arm is not spending money alone. It is spending the sweat of its labourers, the genius of its scientists, and the hopes of its children.[26]

These lines clearly show the human angle of Justice V.R. Krishna Iyer towards common man of the society. Iyer's social justice deals with common man upliftment and development. In the end it can be said that Constitution becomes successful if we have social democracy in the society.

Iyer's Concept of Law

Law is means and justice the end, therefore, the legal process is the bilateral infrastructure of right to justice.[27] But Krishna Iyer says that law is seldom talking term with justice

25. Justice V.R. Krishna Iyer, Equal Justice and Forensic Process, Truth and Myth (1986), p. 101.
26. V.R. Krishna Iyer, Legally Speaking, (2004), p. 34.
27. V.R. Krishna Iyer, Judge Miscellany on Superannuation, (2004), p. 132.

because of the lack of human face in the law. Law must have human face and human feeling and human desire. When man live within the society, he regulates legal Darwinism then he expects the peaceful just and fair society. Then law plays prominent role in making society. Iyer as also supported the human face of law. Therefore, Iyer referring lines of Cardozo—

> Existing rules and principles can give us our present location, our bearing, our latitude and longitude. The inn and shelter for night is not the journey's end. The law, like the traveller must be ready for morrow. It must have a principle of growth.

Rule of law should close the rule of life. Today Indian society suffers from various political, economic and social diseases, but main causes of these problems are due to lack of rule of law in the society. We have the longest Constitution in the world but its practical implementation is nil because of non-supporting behaviour of different section of society. But one thing must be clear that nobody is above the Constitution. Judges are like scientists who dissected the legal rules and norm and make them according to society. Therefore, it can be said that law must have strong vision and preserve social, economic and political philosophy. It is essential requirement of rule of law. Rule of law is essence of democracy and of the Constitution of India. Iyer has referred these words in his book—

> The rule of law is a dynamic concept for expansion and fulfilment of which jurist are primarily responsible and which should be employed not only to safeguard and advance the civil and political rights of individual in a free society, but also to establish social, economic, educational and cultural conditions under which his legitimate aspirations and dignity may realize.[28]

It is clear with the above interpretation that law and rule of law both are different concept. Law is requirement but, it is

28. V.R. Krishna Iyer, Legally Speaking, (2004), p. 149.

not necessary that law is a living organism and deals with harsh realities of human life.

Rule of Law

Law is not machine but human institution. Law and rule of law make the society for well living. One thing must be remembered that, "The winner is always a part of answer. The loser is always a part of the problem, the winner has always a program, the loser has always an excuse.[29]

Law can only make progress in the society when it has human feeling, human desire, human sentiment, and human emotion. Because society is interaction of human feeling and emotions. When law cultivates all these things it becomes the forces than it has became legal Darwinism. If we see the litigation in court, these litigations has human problem and human rights. We can think litigation as problem, but it as human rights and human gravincious Iyer criticize the Indian Legal system because it has chasm between human society and law. Iyer's opinion is that Indian legal system has lack of human face. Therefore, he says that law should deal with socio-economic problem of society. Only then it can serve the purpose. Law does not stand in isolation; it is part of social behaviour of society. Law is a social science.

His Language and Controversy

Language is the vehicle of thoughts. The style of language differs from person to person. Some people use simple language and some use complex. But the language of Justice V.R. Krishna Iyer is not simple but too much difficult to understand. If we study the judgments which are given by Justice V.R. Krishna Iyer then we may found some difficulty to understand. In his judgments sometime he uses the philosophical language and many English prose and poems of different literary persons. Constitutional expert H.M. Servai has criticized Justice V.R. Krishna Iyer for using bombastic words in his judgments. H.M. Servai in his book held that "no more distasteful duty fall to Judge, or to the author of text book on constitutional law, than to criticize judgments for their

29. Verma, J.S., New Dimension of Justice, (2000), p. 106.

style and contents, and not for his or that error in their reasoning. However, it has become an inescapable duty to point out the grave injury done to administration of justice by judgment written in a style which make law laid down uncertain, difficult to understand and difficult to apply."[30]

Even in the field of language, he ought to receive credit for enriching the English language. What is wrong in enriching language by coining new words? Was these words which could express such thought as are conveyed 'by jurisconscience' and social leaper? New thought and new ideas require new words. That is how the language grow, language evolves with thoughts and thoughts are not to imprisoned within the continue of an existing vocabulary. His language is forceful and effective. It succeeds not only in conveying the thought, but also in creating an impact on reader or listener. His massive direction and command on vocabulary make him a master writer and speaker of the English language.[31] Justice Desai, legal doyen Nani Palkiwala has appreciated the language of Justice V.R. Krishna Iyer. In brief it can be said that language used by Justice V.R. Krishna Iyer in his judgments is really tough one. He has vast vision of English literature and original words. In real sense Justice Iyer is true humanist, philosopher, literary person and cultivated man with human passion's feeling and emotions.

Iyer's View Regarding Constitution of India

Justice V.R. Krishna Iyer is of the opinion that the Constitution of India is signature tune of social justice. The Constitution ordains that state is a socialistic state and that all citizens will have economic justice. Social justice depends on economic justice and even political justice is also based on economic justice. Legal realizations have their roots in material condition of life. The preamble of the Constitution of India is a promise of social, economic and political justice and gives stress on directive principles of state policy to create common ownership and distribution of the means of production in the

30. H.M. Servai, Constitutional Law in India, (1983), Vol. III, p. VII.
31. Hari Swarup, For Whom the Law is Made, (1981), p. 29.

hand of common man. Social justice is only possible if we have economic justice.

The concept of state which is given by Justice Krishna Iyer is that of socialistic pattern where all means of production are in the hands of public section and common man. Iyer says that social justice is only pattern of government because in such pattern of government all means are in the hands of the common man. Therefore, he always gave stress on implementation of directive principles of the state policy. Constitution of India deals with common man's conscious but in Iyer's opinion there is need for political implementation of Constitution.

Iyer stress on political implementation of Constitution of India and says that only then social justice is possible in the society. The people of India, through Prime Minister Pandit Jawahar Lal Nehru made tryst with destiny. They resolved that every Indian shall have share in freedom and enjoy the social, economic and political justice together with the fine tuned fundamental rights in a poverty free secular society. But in another place Iyer says that truth to tell, the justice system still has the tenor of the British band and lacks the notes of Bharat's Veena.[32]

Constitution of India is pleasant but there is need to make the conditioning with socio-economic problems of Indian people. No doubt, it is marvelous socio-economic, political or human document but need to implementation.

Justice V.R. Krishna Iyer born as philosopher, became a humanist under socio-economic compulsions, and is jurist by choice. He has deep passion for common man problem. His pro-humanistic approach made him popular among his contemporizes. For him life is not noun, it is verb, it is perennial process not a final product. From him law is not static, but cultural historical motion. Law must change with socio-economic conditions. We cannot implement those laws which prevail in agriculture economy or feudal economy. Nature of the law should be dynamic and progressive in approach.

32. V.R. Krishna Iyer, The Patchy Indian Judicial Record, *The Hindu*, Thursday, Sept., 6, 2007.

The British Crown had jettisoned India from the empire, but colonial law and feudal justice has not been replaced or displayed by dynamic principles of socialistic, secular, democratic justice meeting with raw realities of Indian use. Judicial jurisprudence has not possessed progressive élan of innovative and creative national commitment one who have expected from a system that was administer social and economic justice in the context of penurious humanity reflecting the prembular objectives.[33]

Social justice is only possible when it satisfy needs of common man and the society otherwise it is only paper work and tiger on the pages. Justice is possible if the law satisfy the economic conditions of the society. We have the same laws which are old and unfit to our present society and there is need for revision of these laws. Today the India has entered into 21st century where the intensity of industrialization is austere, but our laws belongs to agriculture economy in those circumstances we cannot expect justice from these laws.

No doubt our constitutional jurisprudence and judicial jurisprudence talks about justice but there is severe need of dynamic and progressive jurisprudence with this legal system. Iyer is of the opinion that there should be progressive and dynamic approach regarding legal system of the society. This study particularly deals with justice Iyer's concept of social justice with special reference to Constitution of India. I divided the whole work in five chapters. First chapter deals with the introduction of social justice. Second chapter discuss Historical development of social justice. Third chapter deals with Directive Principles and Social Justice and its relationship with Fundamental Rights. Fourth chapter discuss Iyer's concept of Social Justice with reference to his judgments and last chapter discuss conclusion of social justice.

Social Justice and Justice V.R. Krishna Iyer

The sublime sentiments, consecrated in the Constitution, is distancing itself from the still sad music of Indian humanity whose life, for considerable numbers, remain a tale of blood,

33. V.R. Krishna Iyer, "The Patchy Indian Judicial Record", *The Hindu*, Thursday, Sept., 6, 2007.

toil, tears and sweet. The great divide between the colonial legal system and free Indian value hidden jurisprudence must be grasped if one is to approach the story of Judicial Development in the domain of Public Interest Litigation.[34] A famous quotation is given by Justice V.R. Krishna Iyer in his book:

> Man's capacity for justice makes democracy possible, but man's inclination to injustice makes democracy necessary.

Justice is not an abstract omnipotence in the sky but an operational causa causans in human affairs. And so, the Judge, the human instrument, the Court, the impersonal apparatus and judiciary, the watch dog institution[35] must never tall below the standard of high credibility, corrective efficiency and inflexible integrity. Alas while among the Principle Engineers of State power the Judicature will keeps the tiner level of culture, the rot has set in even there so much that silence is sin and speech a duty.[36]

Equality of opportunity to all the citizens to develop their individual personalities and to participate in the pleasure and happiness of life is goal of economic justice. Social justice as distinguished from Economic justice has a special significance in the context of Indian society. The term social justice in a comprehensive sense so as to include both economic and social justice. The concept of social justice thus takes within its sweeps the objectives of removing all inequalities and affording equal opportunities to all citizens in social affairs as well as economic activities.[37]

'Social Justice, as I have been at pains to indicate, is a relative concept with changing context dependent on time and circumstances on people culture and aspirations.[38] The Indian

34. Justice V.R. Krishna Iyer, "Off the Bench", Universal Law Publishing Co. Pvt. Ltd., (2005), p. 253.
35. Iyer, V.R. Krishna, "Access to Justice", B.R. Publishing Corporation, Ed., (1993), p. 1.
36. *Id.*, at p. 2.
37. Justice V.R. Krishna Iyer, "Social Justice Sunset or Dawn", Eastern Book Company, 2nd Ed., p. 51.
38. *Op. cit.*, at p. 53.

Constitution says, Granville Austin is first and foremost a social document. The majority of its provisions are either directly aimed at furthering the goals of the social revolution or attempt to foster this revolution by establishing the conditions necessary for the achievement. Yet despite the permeation of the entire Constitution by the aim of National renascence, the core of commitments to the social revolution lies in Part III and IV, in the fundamental rights and in the Directive Principles of State Policy. These are conscious of the Constitution.[39] The Fundamental Rights and Directive Principles had their roots deep in the struggle for independence. And they were included in the Constitution in the hope and exploitation that one day the tree of true liberty would bloom in India. The rights and principles thus connect India's justice, present and past, adding greatly to the significance of their inclusion in the Constitution, and giving strength to the pursuit of social revolution in India.[40] Social Justice is the balancing wheel between freedom, political and economic, and indeed makes for survival of democracy.[41]

The Constitution is our master, has basic structure and fulfils itself only when to every citizen of this land of Daridra Narayana is secured Justice—Social Economic and Political.[42]

According to Justice V.R. Krishna Iyer, social democracy is base of social Justice. Iyer view regarding social Justice is economic one. Without economic justice, social justice not possible. Therefore, there is need of Economic Justice only then social justice can actualize in Indian system. The Indian Constitution has emphasized the only and integrity of the Nation as a paramount value and insisted upon Equality and Dignity as Constitutional Fundamental. It is powerful endeavour to produce classless society, the Constitution has promised Equal Protection.[43]

39. *Op. cit.*, at p. 53.
40. *Op. cit.*, at p. 54.
41. *Op. cit.*, at p. 54.
42. Justice V.R. Krishna Iyer, "Access to Justice", B.R. Publishing Corpn., Ed., (1993), p. 40.
43. Justice V.R. Krishna Iyer, "Dr. Ambedkar and the Dalit Future", B.R. Publishing Corpn., (1990), p. 14.

If you are not a myth
Whose reality are you .
If you are not reality
Whose myth are you

Is Indian Justice a myth or reality or both ? Indian democracy itself is major, illusion wrapped in verbiage and therefore, there is little surprise if its instrumentalities, being but offspring of baloney democracy, share phony qualities. The judiciary can never rise above society itself even as a stream can never rise above its source. If India is only a functioning anarchy so is the judiciary of the country.[44] The Indian justice system, it is universally agreed, thus, a crises of confidence, a stage of terminal illness, a mulish persistence in primitive process, so much so, if survival of the judiciary is desideratum the pathology can be cured only by radical changes.[45]

Appreciating the urgency of quick justice a component of social justice, as a priority item on the Agenda of Law Reforms and suspecting public unawareness of some essential aspect of the problem we make these painful observations. The rule of law and law courts must run close to the rule of life and societal transformation. Otherwise, courts and tribunals would be relegated to the limbs and access to judicial justice an abandoned route.[46]

There must be integral yoga between law and justice. According to Justice V.R. Krishna Iyer social justice is very vast term logy if there is any type of injustice, it means system lack of social justice. While men live within the society, he has many dimensions and needs, fulfilments of those needs desires is social justice.

No country can grow and develop where there is no order, and a society without equal justice will self-destruct.

44. V.R. Krishna Iyer, "Access to Justice", B.R. Publishing Corpn., Ed., (1993), p. 87.
45. *Op. cit.*, p. 92.
46. V.R. Krishna Iyer, "Access to Justice", B.R. Publishing Corpn., Ed., (1993), p. 95.

There must be law and that law must be tempered by Justice. And that Justice must be for all.[47]

Social justice is a long battle and legal soldiers are essential for victory. The integral voga of law and life generates justice.[48] According to Justice V.R. Krishna Iyer, humanism is first essential element to establish the social justice. Social justice çan prevail only in society when human values registered, respected and restored time to time by system. Social justice mean humanity but not legality. Humanity is because of social justice. Social justice can only appeared in the society when there is human or holistic jurisprudence. There is need of militant humanism to establish social justice. Iyer's concept of social justice is based on human values, human moral and human emotions. Nothing is above humanity, is someone denies the humanity it means denial of social justice. Therefore, Justice V.R. Krishna Iyer quoted the following lines:

> There is only one thing in this world, and that is to keep acquiring money and more money, power and more power. All the rest is meaningless.[49]
>
> —*(Hidden Agenda)*

Social justice is the *sine qua non* of the constitutional order. The starting point of all our considerations is poverty or rather a degree of poverty, which means misery, degrades and stultifies the human person and our first task is to recognize and understand the boundaries and limitations which this degrees of poverty imposes. Again, our crudely materialistic philosophy, makes us liable to see only, the material opportunities and overlook immaterial factors. Among the causes of poverty, I am sure, the material factors are entirely secondary such thing as the lack of natural wealth or the lack

47. Justice V.R. Krishna Iyer, Social Justice Sunset or Dawn", Eastern Book Company, (1993), p. 102.
48. Justice V.R. Krishna Iyer, Law, Lawyers and Justice, B.R. Publishing Corpn., Ed., (1988), preface.
49. Quoted in Justice B.R. Krishna Iyer, "Off the Bonch", Universal Publishing, (2005), p. 225.

of capital, or an insufficiency of infrastructure. The primary causes to extreme poverty are immaterial, they lie in certain deficiencies in education, organization and discipline.

> Development does not start with goods, it starts with people and their education organization and discipline. Without these three, all resources remain lateral, untapped potential.[50]

Social Justice is the first charge on our constitutional order. It is a legacy we leave to future generations without tarnishing its purity and power. There are judges who can worthy Redeem this tryst.[51] I am unworthy even to quote with the final words of Cardozo.

The future, gentlemen is your. We have been called to do your parts in ageless process. Long after I am dead and gone, and my little part in it is forgotten you will be here to your share, and to carry the torch forward. I know that the flame will burn bright while the torch is in your keeping.[52]

Indeed, the third world jurisprudence can serve social justice only if the methodology of draftsmanship and rules to statutory interpretation undergo charge. Even the legal professions which great mediator between Court and the community must come closer to cause of the common man, of human justice and of human law.[53]

Working of social justice means abolishing the eternal conflict between capital and labour. If the rule of law and the rule of life run close together, a jurisprudence where the man matters will bourgon there. The springs of social Justice will rise then only then. Social Justice is people's justice where the tyranny of power is transferred into social good.[54] There is need of Constitution militancy to establish the social justice in

50. *Ibid.*, p. 247.
51. Justice B.R. Krishna Iyer, "Access to Justice", B.R. Publishing Corporation, Ed., (1993), p. IX.
52. *Op. cit.*, p. X.
53. *Op. cit.*, p. 97.
54. Justice V.R. Krishna Iyer, "Social Justice Sunset or Dawn", Eastern Law Company, 2nd Ed., p. 18.

India. Social Justice is a militant thought for establishing justice in society. Because future belongs to life not to death. Present troubles are the future destiny. Our Constitution respects the dignity and, therefore, the divinity of individual and preservation of life of every one's life.[55] Social Justice is not only an Indian but a global struggle and is not so much against judicial inhumanity as against exploitative society.

Iyer's concept of social Justice is very vast and comprehensive in its sense. Therefore, concept of social justice is deeply rooted in humanism. Without humanism there is no exploitation of social justice in every phase of country.

Law is a human institution created by human agents to serve human ends said Harlon Fiske Stone and Jawaharlal Nehru put the point Pithily when he said that rule of law must run close to rule of life.[56] A legal order cannot endure without a constitutional control system regulating and directing the organs of power. The peaceful co-existence of the constitutional instrumentalities and upset when tensions develops unprovided for situation arise and scheme envisaged by the fundamental law is thrown out of year. Constitutionalism is deeper than the letter of the Constitution. No satisfactory resolution of conflict is possible merely through laws even Constitutional Law. For, law limps in this area without the backing of enlightened national consensus so that therapeutic measures must be legal and para-legal, through new corrective agencies and convention with teeth. The ultimate guardian of the Law is not the policeman or the judge, but public opinion, informed by new value system and aware of perils of constitutional disorder. So we cannot thinks solely of legislative manipulation and must organize other method too older caution but younger values, complex and flexible means to vet new conflict such is the sweep of constitutional technology.[57]

55. Justice V.R. Krishna Iyer, Law, Lawyer and Justice, B.R. Publishing Coprn., p. 83.
56. V.R. Krishna Iyer, Social Mission of Law, Orient Longman Ltd., First Published (1978), p. 76.
57. *Op. cit.*, pp. 63-64.

But in India, the Judiciary keep itself largely ivory towered, and cut-off from the community, seeking refuge in traditional judicial isolationism even when on subject of law and legal procedure where they have professional expertise, their valuable opinion is sought by the state or the Law Commission.[58]

58. *Op. cit.*, p. 70.

2

Historical Development of the Concept of Social Justice

INTRODUCTION

Social justice is not a new concept, it has deep historical development. This concept is said to be as old as human civilization. Man is social animal when he lives within the society; he expects that he should be treated equally. Different philosophers and thinkers of the world have propounded different philosophy of social justice, which are based on the economic condition of that time. But basic of these philosophies is the development of human being. Social justice is totally humanistic approach towards the society and living beings. And socio-economic conditions changed, this concept has also changed, but basic has remained same.

As civilization made progress and democracy came into existence, this concept became popular. Today in the era of constitutionalism every government has given different provisions regarding social justice in their Constitution. Indian Constitution is also based on the concept of social, economic and political justice.

Under the Constitution of India social justice, in fact, concern itself with rights of social rather than a personal nature, the rights which are individuals share in common with the society rather than exercise individually.

> "Social Justice is a balance between social rights and social control, in a manner that neither the right nor the control should go into an excess!

The Constitution of India is social document. Under the Constitution, Directive Principles of State Policy promise social, economic and political justice. These principles are based on the social good, social welfare or social and economic development at large.

The concept of social justice is also enshrined in our fundamental rights. When Constitution of India speaks about no discrimination shall be made on the basis of caste, sex, race, place of birth, religion, etc. In this way, Constitution of India is a social document which is based on human development.

Meaning of Social Justice

> "The concept of social Justice thus takes within its sweeps the objective removing all inequalities and affording equal opportunities to all citizen in social affairs as well as Economic activities".[1]

The origin of the concept of social justice is traced by modern jurists from the time of formation of International Labour Organization after end of World War I. There has been a historical process through this concept which was initially a doctrine of social philosophy and entered into state craft, and captured the constitutional field. The Glorious Revolution of 1688 in England with its achievement of the Bill of Rights, the American War of Independence with its fruition in 1776, The French Revolution with success in the Declaration of Rights of

1. L.M. Singvi, "Law of Poverty", ed., 1973, p. 15.

Men (1789) and the Russian Revolution of 1917.[2] All these Revolutions based on the social justice. Social justice is subject to compromise between two classes.

The society consisted of two classes, the privilege of and unprivileged. Dr. Chaturvedi rightly observed that it was through vehicle of Revolution that this concept becomes a political settlement. The Constitution being changed, the Revolutionary minds thought it wiser to secure this concept a place of pride and performance by engrafting some of its vital features in draft of their respective Constitution. The concept which was originally a social exhortation thus culminated into a legal document.[3]

Social Justice is the signature tune of our Constitution. Our Constitution talks about social justice and the welfare of the citizens. Glanville Austin thinks of Indian Constitution when he describes it as embodying the essence of social justice. He says, majority of provisions deals with social order or social welfare. Preamble of Indian Constitution starts with five great words, We the People of India Solemnly Resolved Constitute Sovereign Socialistic. The Democratic Republic and Justice of Social, Economic and Political.

It is the preamble which reflects the real mind of the maker of the Constitution. It is the preamble which envisages the Indian Constitution is the combination of both the elements of democracy and socialism. The preamble starts with the phrase "we the people of India having solemnly resolved to constitute India into sovereign democratic republic and to secure to all its citizen justice, social, economic and political liberty of thought, expression, belief faith and worship equality of status and opportunity and to promote among them all fraternity assuming the dignity of the individuals and the unity of the nation. The phrase we the people of India talks the Indian people sovereign master while the words democratic only the Constitution assures the citizen social economic political justice without any discrimination. The maker of the Constitution knew it well that democracy without social

2. *Ibid.*, at p. 15.
3. S.S. Prakash, "Bonded Labour and Social Justice", Ed., 1990, p. 30.

economic justice has no meaning. It is social justice which put every Indian on equal footing in the society protect his social status. The economic justice saves the poor and downtrodden section of the people from economic exploitation and entitles them to get the national benefit yielded by the effort of the government through various economic means.[4]

Equality means in India equal opportunity to every one in all walks of life. Dr. Ambedkar while speaking in the Constitution assembly rightly said that sole purpose of preamble had to constitute a new society in India based on the liberty and equality, socialism word has been added in the preamble by 42nd Amendment. But by adding the word you cannot bring socialism and social justice in the society, for this there must be some basic change in economy or social system.

Directive principle of state policy directs the government to create such society. That is why Directive Principles of State Policy is based on the concept of social justice, social revolution and social development. Directive Principles gives the direction to make balance between the interest of individual and society. That is why Mr. Issac Advocate says that:

> Social Justice connotes the balance of adjustment of various interests, concerned in the social and economic structure of the state in order to promote harmony upon an ethical and economic basis.[5]

In case Justice Gajendragadkar define social justice in *Central Bank of India* vs. *Raj Gopalan,* AIR 1964, P 742, the concept of social justice is not narrow or one sided and pedantic, and is not confined to industrial adjudication alone, its sweeps is comprehensive. It is founded on the basic ideal of socio-economic equality and its aim is to assist the removal of social-economic disparities and inequalities.[6]

Justice Iyer says that the concept of social justice mean remove all type of inequalities in social affair as well as economic affairs.

---

4. Chandrika Singh, "Constitutional Battle in India", ed., 2001, p. 36.
5. S.N. Johari, "Industrial Jurisprudence", ed., 1984, p. 140.
6. AIR 1964 SC 742 para 19.

The vice of social inequalities assume particularly reprehensible form in revaluation to the backward classes and communities which are treated as untouchable's and so the problem of social justice is an urgent and important in India as is the problem of economic justice.

Justice V.R. Krishna Iyer, *Mumbai Kamghar Sabha* v. *M/s. Abdul Bhai Tai Zullah Bhai,* AIR 1976 SC 1455 tries to extend the sweep of social justice over produced technicalities when he says that "our adjectival branch of jurisprudence, by and large, deals not with sophisticated litigants but the rural poor, the urban lay on weaker social segment for when the law will be an added terror if technical misdescription and deficiencies in drafting pleading and setting out cause little create secret weapon to non suit a latitude in grace of processural justice.

Social justice means removal of all type of inequalities and discriminations in the society. Social justice is totally pro-humanistic approach. Social justice upholds the human value and human feeling and emotions. That is why social justice is the most fascinating term for every man. All the constitutions of world are based on the social justice. It means that we cannot do anything against human being without reason. Social justice shall always be regarded to human dignity and want to abolish all type of exploitation in field of human relationship. A human being is that terminology which based on equality, liberty. It is totally humanistic approach. Social justice gives the stress to effective use of human right and effect implication of legal system.

2.1 ANCIENT WESTERN THOUGHTS ON CONCEPT OF SOCIAL JUSTICE

The concept of social justice has its deep roots in legal history of Greek. Many thinkers have given contribution in the development of this concept.

Plato (429-387 B.C.)

Plato was one of the greatest philosophers of the world. He discussed the concept of justice in his book 'The Republic'. Justice meant in Plato's eyes that, a man should do his work in station of life to which he was called by his capacities. Every member of society, according to him, has his specific functions and should confine his activity to the proper discharge of these functions. Some people have power to command, the capacity to govern others are capable of helping those in power to achieve their ends as subordinate members of the government.[7]

Plato divided the society in three different parts. On the top were the men of gold who become ruler and they must be philosopher. The second one was man of silver which were doing work of military and third men of iron which were producing class. Plato was of the opinion that these were (ruler, soldiers and artisans) symbol of reason, spirit and temperance and justice is fourth element in society.

Plato's concept of social justice was based on the concept of each according to his ability and each according to his need. Plato says that justice is real foundation of society. No society exist without just system. He also talks about communism about property. He wanted to abolish the concept of private property. In brief it can be said that his concept of social justice is based on communistic pattern of society.

Aristotle (384-322 B.C.)

Aristotle was a disciple of Plato, Aristotle was in favour of rule of law that is why he talked about rule of government not the rule of man. His concept about social justice was radical one. He divided justice into two parts universal justice and particular justice and, the later was divided into distributive justice and corrective justice.[8]

Universal justice means complete virtue. Universal justice means equal implementation of all laws in society. Particular justice means which deals with particular law for example criminal, etc. Distributive justice is exercised in the distribution of honour, wealth and other divisible assets of the community which may allot among its members in equal or unequal share.[9]

7. Edgar Boden Heimer, Jurisprudence, (2001), p. 7.
8. Crains, Huntington to Legal Philosophy from Plato to Hegal, 1967, p. 122.
9. *Ibid.*

Corrective justice is rule of arithmetical proportion and is a matter for judiciary. Corrective justice is with judge's power to decide the matter. Corrective justice brings equality between parties.

Aristotle's concept of social justice essentially deals with equal distribution of gods among people and wanted to make balance of interest between different sections of people.

Cicero

Cicero believed that justice was supreme virtue of society. Justice is defined by Cicero that sentiment which assigns to each own and maintain with generosity and equity of human solidarity and alliance.[10] Cicero divided the law into three parts. Divine law, eternal law and human law. But according to Cicero human made law cannot bring justice in the society because man always made the law for his own advantage. That is why he believed in divine law. According to Cicero divine law is only just, good and creates justice-based society. Cicero was philosopher of Natural Law School. Cicero was in favour of equal law, i.e. law based on equality.

Cicero's jurisprudence embraced a humanitarian ideal which was vital from for many centuries which is still influential. He holds that men of high moral character were made King in order that people might enjoy the justice.[11] His concept of social justice was based on equality.

2.2 RELIGIOUS THINKERS AND CONCEPT OF SOCIAL JUSTICE

St. Thomas Acquinas and St. Augustine comes under the purview of religious thinkers.

Thomas Aquinas (1226-74)

St. Thomas Aquinas said that Justice is habit whereby man render to each one of his due by constant and perpetual will. Its fundamental idea is some kind of equality and

10. *Id.*, p. 161.
11. *Ibid.*

therefore, it is proper to justice to direct man in his relation to other.[12]

The Thomastic conception of justice, strongly show the influence of Cicero and Aristotle. According to Aquinas justice is of two types, distributive justice and cumulative justice. Consequently in distributive justice a person receives all the more of common goods according to holds a more prominent position in community. In corrective justice, on the other hand it is necessary to equalize things with their arithmetical fashion, so that who's suffered by some one as result of harmful act can be restored and unjust enrichment of the party of the expenses of another can be rectified.[13]

St. Thomas Aquinas concept of social justice is based on everyone gets his due. Therefore, he talks about distributive or cumulative justice.

2.3 THE CLASSICAL ERA AND CONCEPT OF SOCIAL JUSTICE

During Middle Ages the Church was centre of life in Europe. Church controlled human life and was also a decisive factor for society's development. During that period natural law philosophy was prevalent. At that time Hugo Gortius, Hobbs, Locke Rousseau were philosophers of classical era or Natural Law School.

Hugo Grotius (1583-1645)

Grotius was father of international law and also supporter of natural law school. Grotius defined law as "a dictate of right reason which point out that an act according as it is or is not in conformity with rational nature has a quality of moral baseness or moral necessity."[14]

Grotius used the construction of social contract for two-fold purpose, internally for justification of the absolute duty of obedience of people to the government, internationally to

12. *Id.*, p. 196.
13. Edgar Bodenheimer, Jurisprudence, (2001), p. 26.
14. *Ibid.*, p. 35.

create a basis for legally binding and stable relation among state.[15]

Grotius social contract, which creates duty of government towards people and government, will make balance between the right and duties of citizens. By this contract balance has also been created between King and citizens. Balance of interests was the basis of social contract theory.

Thomas Hobbes (1588-1679)

Thomas Hobbes was also profounder of social contract theory. Hobbes wrote his principal book De Cive (1642) and Laviathan (1667) with definite political purpose. According to Hobbes in state of nature every man was brutish or selfish by nature for property matter.

With the passage of time social contract has been made between the subjects. Contract has not been made between subject and sovereign but only between subjects. Sovereign is not party to contract. In this conception of social contract the sovereign cannot commit the breach of covenant, because he is not party to it.[16]

Hobbes, by this contract talks about absolute sovereignty of King. But Hobbes social contract reveals one thing that he wants to make balance of interest. According to Hobbes both man in society want equality in hope for attaining our ends but both men cannot attain their ends they can become enemies of each other, therefore, there should be balance between interests of both men. According to Hobbes competition, secondly diffidence, thirdly, glory was cause of quarrel within society. But by this social contract every man has right to everything and even to another body social justice can be brought only by social contract between different sections of society by putting limitations over right of each other.

Locke (1632-1704)

Locke was also supporter of social contract theory and also in the favour of legal sovereignty. His political theory

15. W. Friedman, Legal Theory (1999), p. 19.
16. William Friedman, Great Political Thinker, (1975), p. 360.

gave power expression to aspirations and interests of class which was defined to lad to profit not from emancipation for long time to come.[17]

According to Locke two contracts have been made one with subject and second with King or State. King will protect the right of individuals in the society. His theory has made greatest effect on French revolution and American Revolution. These revolutions were fought for democratic rights. Equal freedom and fraternity were bases of these revolutions. According to Locke base of social contract provide social justice to the society.

Rousseau (1712-88)

Rousseau was in favour of popular sovereignty. He gave concept of general will. In his social contract theory he wrote, "Man is born free but every where in chain." His social contract theory supports the natural right.[18]

In civil society, the individual is subject to no other individual but merely "to the general will", 'volante general' that is will community. In this will interest of state and king should not contrary to subjects. Rousseau's General will is based of democratic process. If the King does anything against subject, then subject has right to recall the king. According to Rousseaus, General will was based on the social consciousness and social justice.

Benthem (1748-76)

Benthem was father of utility theory. Utility was defined by Benthem "that principle which approves or disapproves of every action whatever, according to tendency which it appears to have to argument or diminish the happiness of the party whose interest is in question.[19]

The business of government according to Benthem was to promote happiness to society by furthering the enjoyment of pleasure and affording security against pain.[20]

17. W. Friedmen, Legal Theory, (1999), p. 129.
18. William Ebsitin, Great Political Thinkers, (1975), p. 367.
19. Edgar Bodenheimer, Jurisprudence, (2001), p. 85.
20. *Ibid.*

According to Benthem society has four goals—subsistence, abundance, equality and security. Benthem's concept was based on greatest good of greatest number. Although he was supporter of *laissez faire* and wanted freedom in economic sphere.

2.4 SOCIOLOGICAL THINKERS AND SOCIAL JUSTICE

Roscoe Pound

Sociological jurisprudence is based on the balance of interest. Pound was founder of American sociological jurisprudence. According to him there are three types of interests in the society.

(1) Individual Interest
(2) Public Interest
(3) Social Interest

Poundian theory wants to make balance between three interests. Main function of law is to create balance between these interests. His theory is based on these lines "to satisfy maximum wants with minimum frictions and wastage.

2.5 ECONOMIC THINKERS AND CONCEPT OF SOCIAL JUSTICE

Different economic thinkers have also contributed for the development of this concept. Economic equality is main pillar of social justice.

Marxian View of Social Justice (1818-83)

Karl Heinrich Marx is one of the most important and influential political thinker. In comprehending the major thrust of his political philosophy directed towards human liberation, one to take note of the significant shift that took place in human thinking in the late sixteenth country when the traditional paradigm of analyzing political order on the basis of scarcity was replaced by a philosophy of abundance.[21] Most

21. V.P. Verma, "Ancient and Medieval Indian Political thought", Lakshmi Narayan Aggarwal, Revised 2005, p. 277.

of the communistic countries are regulated by the thinking of this great saint of world. Today people think that this ideology is going to die but ideas never die but their shape change time to time with pressure of socio-economic condition. Marx believed in scientific humanism.

Economic condition determines human nature. Marxian philosophy of social justice is based on the concept of equal distribution of economic resources among society. In capitalistic pattern of society social justice is not possible. But in communistic pattern of society social justice is reality because in such pattern everybody gets according to his need and each according to capacity, Marx was also of the opinion that means of production determine human nature. Therefore, he divided human history in five stages—

(1) Primitive Stage
(2) Feudalism
(3) Capitalism
(4) Socialism
(5) Communism

Marx was of the opinion that there must be socialization of means of production. Only then social justice is possible. Marxian thesis regarding social justice is based on each according to necessity and each according to his ability.

Pigou

Pigou's welfare economy is based on maximum welfare of society. According to Pigou economic policy should be of such type which brings social development in society. Pigou about welfare economics says that I did not speak of these things, but confine myself to aspect of welfare associated with economic circumstances; and I conceived of economic welfare as satisfaction and dissatisfaction derived from these circumstances depending for community, partly on size of its real income, partly on was in which this was allocated among individuals.[22]

22. William Ebsitin, Great Political Thinkers, (1975), p. 837.

2.6 HINDU JURISPRUDENCE AND THE CONCEPT OF SOCIAL JUSTICE

The Hindu jurisprudence is regulated by concept of dharma. The concept of dharma resemble with modern concept of rule of law. The term dharma is a derived term from the Sanskrit root 'dhri' which means uphold, to sustain or to nourish.[23] "Dharma is that which sustains and ensures progress and welfare of all in this world and eternal bliss in other world. The dharma is promulgated in term of commands."[24] Dharma means good conduct. In ancient India the strength of the dharma was in public acceptance. In ancient India the strength of the Dharma was in public acceptance. The entire Indian philosophy is based on concept of dharma. Five fundamental rules of Dharma have been given in Manusmriti. Ahimsa, Satya, Asteya, Shocham and Indryanigraha are in brief the common elements of dharma.[25] Dharma means society regulated by good conduct or morality. Dharma has highest place under Hindu jurisprudence. In England King can do no wrong but Hindu jurisprudence says that if the King do anything wrong, he shall also be punishable under dharma. The supremacy of dharma was declared thus—

> Law is King of Kings; nothing is superior to law; the law aided by the power of the King enables the weak to prevail over strong.[26]

Dharma and concept of social justice both are correlated to each other. It is the duty of King to perform the welfare function for the development of common man. Equality is based on concept of dharma. The character of equality has been incorporated in Vedas. Indian Hindu jurisprudence has four great Vedas and 17 Puranas. These Vedas and Puranas deal with the concept of dharma, equality and social justice. In Rigveda equality is discussed in this way.

---

23. U.C. Sarkar, Epoch in Hindu History, 1958, p. 19.
24. Rama Jois, Seeds of Modern Public Law in Ancient Indian Jurisprudence, (2000), p. 8.
25. *Id.*, p. 10.
26. *Id.*, p. 24.

> No one is superior or inferior. All are brothers. All should strive for interest of all and should progress collectively.[27]

Again in Atharveda, Sanjanansukta, the right of individual in respect of natural resources was declared.

> All have equal rights on articles of food and water. The yoke of the chariot of life is placed equally on the shoulders of all. All should live together with harmony supporting one another like the spokes of a wheel of the chariot connecting its rim and hub.[28]

Our Vedas and ancient Puranas express deep support for social justice or equality. Duty of King was to protect and support all his subjects without any discrimination. On thing is revealed that concept of social justice was deep rooted in our noble heritage in Vedas and human values.

2.7 ANCIENT INDIAN THINKERS AND CONCEPT OF SOCIAL JUSTICE

Manusmriti and Concept of Social Justice

Manusmriti or Manu dharmasasthra, which we call Code of Manu, is much more celebrated than any other smriti. As sources of dharma it is classed in India at the head of all smriti, immediately after the Veda.[29]

In Manusmriti, concept of dharma has assigned duty on King that he shall not make any discrimination for welfare of people. King shall follow dharma. Dharma is above the King. If he fails to follow dharma then he shall be punishable. In Manusmriti IX 311 says that:

> The King should support his entire subject without any discrimination in the manner as earth supports all living beings.[30]

27. *Id.*, p. 49.
28. *Id.*, p. 50.
29. Robert Lingat, The Classical Law of India, (1998), p. 71.
30. Rama Jois, Seeds of Modern Public Law, (2000), p. 57.

Equality and non-discrimination was based on Manusmriti. Manusmriti discussed that King shall always function in conformity with dharma or equality. Equality and equal protection of law are necessary for all human beings. The reflection of this can found in the provisions regarding administration of justice which dwelt with later. Further, these provisions of dharma are incorporated in terms of fundamental right to equality in Articles 14, 15, 16, 17 of the Constitution of India.[31]

In Manusmriti welfare of people has been elaborately discussed by Manu. King's duty is to perform the functions towards the welfare of people and create such type of social order which makes maximum development of citizens. Today in our Constitution, directive principles of state policy are based on the welfare of subject and social justice to citizens.

Manusmriti has also elaborated procedural or substantive law. When the King gave justice he had to take opinion of court. If King was unable to perform his function then court will preside the seat of King for administration of justice. But while deciding the matter the concept of dharma should be kept in mind. Today we talk about rule of law; this rule of law came from the concept of dharma.

Non-discrimination, equality and liberty are basis of Manusmriti.

Kautilya and Social Justice

The Arthsasthra was treated in ancient time as an independent subject dealing with political, constitutional, judicial and administrative matters. In his book Kautilya has assigned duty on the King that King shall bring about well-being and security of subject which consists in protecting his subject with justice; its observance leads him to heaven. One who does not protect his people or who inflict unjust punishment, wields his happiness, their welfare is his own welfare; he shall not consider what please and benefit him personally, but what is pleasing and beneficial to the people.[32]

31. *Ibid.*
32. V.K. Gupta, Kautilyan Jurisprudence, (1987), p. 16.

The King shall not make any discrimination with subjects. Kautilyan concept of social justice speaks that King should do all work for welfare of subjects. It is duty of King to provide justice to the subjects.

In Arthsashtra Kautilya also discussed the welfare activities such as, maintenance of orphans, aged, helpless man, women or newly born child. It was the duty of the King to provide facilities to his section of society. These things show that Kautilya was in favour of social justice to these persons of the society.

Ramayana, Mahabharata and Concept of Social Justice

Mahabharata is not only a great epic but an encyclopedic account of various philosophical opinion prevalent in Ancient India. The Mahabharata chiefly embraces instructions as to duties of Kings and the military class.[33] In the same position of the Manushastra, we see another version of a social contract by which the people receive protection term the King and render on their part, obedience. The King is to advance the good of his subjects temporarily and spiritually, and in consideration thereof is to receive not only worldly good but also high spiritual merits.[34]

Ramayana and Mahabharata are great epics of Indian Hindu jurisprudence. The authors of these two works Valmiki and Vyasa were of outstanding merits, which are held in highest esteem by Indian society. They have incorporated the most important principle of dharma which was accepted and prevailing in the society in their respective ages in the context in which they became relevant while narrating stories.[35]

In Ramayana we see the concept of dharma accepted by society. There are as many as 66 versus in Ramayana which deal with Rajdharma and duties of Kings towards their people and subjects.[36]

In Mahabharata there are about 100 couples which deal with Kingdom and concept of dharma. Moreover, Gita talks

33. H.S. Bhatia, "Political, Legal and War Philosophy" in Ancient India, Deep & Deep Publications Pvt. Ltd. ed., 2001, p. 62.
34. *Op. cit.*, at p. 65.
35. Rama Jois, Legal and Constitutional History of India, (1990), p. 39.
36. *Id.*, p. 39.

about equality of human beings. The message given by Lord Krishna to Arjun for fighting war was based on the concept of dharma.

Various ancient Indian thinkers Kabira, Rahim, Goswami Tulsidas, Valmiki, and Guru Nanak Dev have supported concept of Justice.

Kabira

Kabira's social or humanistic approach wanted to create a civilized society. Saint Kabir was a social reformer who took voice against various social evils. Social vision of Kabir wanted to establish a justice-based society where, there is no discrimination. He wanted to establish classless and socialistic pattern of society. Kabir has written these lines :

बनाई बस क कजिए जौ मन नहि तजै बिकार।
घर–बन ससरि जिमि किआ ते विरजा संसार
का जटा भसम लेपन कि ये कहा गुफा में बास
मन जीते जग जीतिए, जौ बिरि या तै रहै उदास।।[37]

He wanted to abolish all social and economic evils. If we make analysis of Kabir literature then we shall definitely find that he wanted to provide social, economic justice to the society. These lines of Kabira says whole story:

साई इतना दीजियै, जामैं कुटुम समाय
मैं भी भूखा ना रहुं साधु ना भूखा जाये ।[38]

Kabira gives stress on the personal contentment of man. He wanted to create social consciousness among human beings. According to Kabira if we realize ourselves then there is no need for anything, all social evils, injustice, exploitation will come to an end. Kabira was always against the caste system.

37. श्री शरन, कबीर व्यक्तित्व और अस्तित्व, (2001), पृ० 69 ।
38. वही, पृ० 69 ।

Goswami Tulsidas

Goswami Tulsidas was also against caste system. In his various writings he said the Brahman and Kashtriya should have the minimum desires and he laid down on the development of low castes. According to Goswami Tulsidas a person is low or Shudra due to lack of education of power. If they get all these things then there is no lower of upper class in the society. He says that king should perform functions in the favour of subjects and should provide the equal justice to this section of society. His social vision was based on the social justice.[39]

Guru Nanak Dev (1469 to March 10, 1538)

Nanak was a great theist and he had an emancipated mind. As a Khatri he taught against the caste arrogance of the Brahmanical Priest and denounced their ritualism and idolatry. Nanak to the extent that he denounced the caste system. Nanak was also non-Brahamin. According to Nanak Dev, God is true, the srentor, devoid of fear and envy, immortal, unborn, self-existent, great and bountiful. According to him the soul attain the finality according to deed performed by it.[40]

Guru Nanak Dev was born in the 15th century in the plains of Punjab, now forming part of Pakistan. Guru Nanak was one of torch bearers of the so-called modern age, though in the case of India, the medieval age continued upto the 18th century.[41] He was against caste system. He talks about the concept of roti or beti. That method can solve all problems in the society. Guru Nanak had humanistic approach towards society. He also laid stress on self-realization. He says that if you know 'thyself you shall be free. These following lines of Guru Nanak give the true picture of human being.

Self-assertion give man his individuality leads him to action, it also lays him to down to earth to the world and send him on a rounds of rebirths and death where from come the assertion of self ? How does it have ? It comes to man from will of God and determines his conduct according to his

39. Wazir Singh, Humanism of Guru Nanak, (1977), p. 1.
40. Harold Laski, "A Grammer of Politics Anamika Publisher, p. 47.
41. आचार्य रामचन्द्र शुक्ल, गोस्वामी तुलसीदास, (2004), पृ0 40.41

antecedents. It is great disease, but its remedy also lies within itself.[42]

Saint Ravi Das

Saint Ravi Das was also against caste system. In his various song saint Ravi Das said that there should no discrimination on the basis of caste. He wanted to abolish all type of social economic disparities. Saint Ravi Das gives stress on self-satisfaction and contentment. He said that man is not measure by material things but by his action.

Saint Ravi Das wants to establish casteless classless society. He always talked about the social economic equality.

His social vision was based on the social or economic justice. During his life he started movement against caste systems.

Saint Ravi Das was a true social reformer. He has taken voice against social discrimination. That is why; he talked about the social equality and economic equality in the society.

2.8 JUDICIAL SYSTEM AND CONCEPT OF SOCIAL JUSTICE

Ancient Hindu judicial system was regulated by concept of Dharma. The judicial system and the concept of social justice are discussed hereunder.

Constitution of Court

In Ancient India the King was regarded as the fountain of justice. His foremost duty was to protect his subject. He was respected as the Lord of Dharma with supreme authority of administration in his kingdom. The King's court was highest court of appeal as well as original court in case of vital importance of state. The King's court was advised by learned Brahmin, the Chief Justice and other judges, ministers, elders and representatives of trading community.[43]

42. Wazir Singh, Humanism of Guru Nanak, (1977), p. 67.
43. V.D. Kulashashtra, Landmark of Indian Legal and Court History, (1981), p. 6.

Punishment

Ancient punishment method was based on God faith and religious norms as the punishment was dealt with as under :

Ordeal by balance
Ordeal by fire
Ordeal by water
Ordeal by poison
Ordeal by lot
Ordeal by rice grain
Ordeal by fountain (king)

Ordeal by Balance

According to this method the accused was put on the weighting scale come down of the person then it was presumed that he had committed the crime if the scale increased then he was considered to be innocent.

Ordeal by Fire

If the accused could cross the fire without any harm to him then he was considered to be innocent.

Ordeal by Water

By this condition the accused has to sit under water for particular time. If he had completed that time then he was presumed to be innocent.

Ordeal by Poison

It was based on the god faith. A person had to drink poison, if the person survived after drinking that poison the person was considered to be innocent.

Ordeal by Lot

By this proposition two lots were given to the person, one was symbol of dharma and other was adharma. If the person drew the dharma lot then he was considered to be innocent.

Ordeal by Rice Grains

The accused was required to chew unhusked rice and then was asked to spit out. If traces of blood appeared in his mouth then he was considered guilty.

Ordeal by Fountain

The king would give the water to accused; by drinking this water accused confess his guilt.[44]

Islamic Approach to Social Justice

The Islamic History is replete with glorious anecdotes in which the ideal of administration of social justice implemented. In Quran:

> O Believers ! Stand firmly with God as
> Your witness for fair dealing among people,
> You hatred of people should not seduce you
> To commit a wrong or depart from justice;
> For justice is next to piety (5:8)
>
> O Believers ! Stand out firmly for justice as
> Witness to God—even if it be against yourselves
> Your parent or your kin and whether it be
> Against rich of poor (4 : 135)

These verses from Quran uphold, in unambiguous terms, an ideal vision of justice. They exhort and enjoin man stand firmly on the side of justice.[45]

The Quran further admonishes the Muslim not to deviate from the path of justice even when the adversary is their bitter enemy, or belongs to people hostile to Islam.[46]

God will not change the prosperous state of people unless they first change their own heart and selves. (8:53)

And why should you not fight in the cause of God and for those men, women and children who being weak are ill-treated and oppressed. (4:75)

Because the whole world, creation itself, is the target of the Muslim will to transform and refashion, the community of Islam is the human race in its totality. Here every man is citizen and everyone count. None is excluded virtue of his/her

---

44. V.D. Kulashashtra, Landmark of Indian Legal History, (1981), p. 10.
45. Dr. K.K. Usman, This is Islam, (1998), p. 54.
46. *Ibid.*

progeny, colour religion culture. Man's humanness constitutes his full candidacy for membership.[47]

But we cannot comprehend the nature of social justice in Islam until we have first studied the Islamic concept of Divinity, the universe, life and humanity. For social justice is only a branch of the great principle on which all Islamic teachings are based.[48]

On the other hand Island also claim that if man will follow the principle it has laid down, Allah will be with him, but the main condition is that man must act with unqualified faith, for his success, in Allah. It claims to offer a contented life, a perfect economic system, or more accurately a basis therefore, that is founded on social justice and equality of man, which could certainly increase our joy in living.[49] Wealth, therefore, would become a means and not an end in itself, and there need be no shame from the thought that so many are denied, through poverty, an access to the means of happiness that rich possess, because they would meet their obligation if they believe in Allah.[50]

For one thing, it is comprehensive human justice embracing all sides and basic factor of human life. It is not merely a limited economic justice. It, therefore, deals with all aspect of life and its activities, even as it is concerned with mind and attitude, with heart and conscience. The values with which this justice deals are not only economic values, nor are they merely material values in general; rather they are mixture of these values, and moral, and spiritual value together.[51]

Islam looks at man as forming unity whose spiritual aspirations cannot be separated from his bodily desires, and whose spiritual needs cannot be divorced from his material needs. It looks at the universe and at life with this all embracing view which permits so separation of division.

Secondly, in the Islamic view, life consists of established, well defined form of mutual love, and respect, co-operation

47. *Ibid.*, p. 54.
48. Khurshid Ahmed, Islam, its Meaning and Message, (1977), p. 118.
49. Syed Ahmed Ali, Economic Foundation of Islam, (1964), p. 142.
50. *Ibid.*, p. 143.
51. Khurshid Ahmed, Islam, its Meaning and Message, (1977), p. 12.

and mutual responsibility between Muslim particular between all human being general.

There are two main features—the absolute, just and coherent unity and general, mutual responsibility of individuals and societies, by which marked the concept of social justice in Islam, which takes into consideration the basic element of human nature, and does not, at the same time, disregard human abilities.[52] At the same time Islam does not ignore the needs and the welfare of society, no does it overlook the high ideals of life both in individual and society in every age and among different people.

Justice in Islam is human equality envisaging the adjustment of all values, of which the economic forms a part. To be precise, justice in Islam means equality in opportunity and freedom of talents which look within the limits that do not come into conflict with the high ideals of life. Islam also recognizes the claims of poor upon the wealth of the rich, according to their needs, and to the same extent as is suitable for society; and thus guarantees its equivalence, balance and growth. As such Islam does not neglect any of the various aspect of life material intellectual, religious and worldly.[53]

The foundations of the Islamic value of equality are deeply rooted in the structure of Islam. It stems from basic principles such as following:

1. All men are created equally by one and same eternal God, the supreme lord of all.
2. All mankind belong to human race and share equally in common parentage of Adam and Eve.
3. God is just and kind to all his creatures. He is not partial, biased against a race, nation, age, sex. The whole universe is his dominion and all people are his creatures.
4. All people born equal in the sense that they take back nothing of their worldly belonging.
5. God judges every person on the basis of his/her own merits and according to his own deeds.

52. Khurshid Ahmed, Islam, its Meaning and Message, (1977), p. 126.
53. *Ibid.*, pp. 129-30.

6. God has conferred on man, as human being, a title of honour and dignity.[54]

In the end it can be said that Islam is based on Humanism, social justice and equality.

British Era and Concept of Social Justice

British came in India for economic imperialism. They wanted to earn maximum profit rather than to provide social service and social justice to the society. They wanted to utilize economic resources of India.

Indian Constitutional Development and Socio-Economic Justice

The Indian National Congress was founded in December 1885. The Indian desire for civil rights was implicit in its formation.[55] Indians wanted same rights as were enjoyed by Britishers.

Perhaps the earliest demand for recognition of fundamental rights commanded with the Constitution of India Bill, 1895 probably issued under inspiration of Lokmanya Bal Gangadhar Tilak has described as Home Rule Bill by Annie Basant.[56]

In 1906 Congress demanded self-rule with a view that only Swaraj can help to get rid of economic ills.

In 1909 Minto Morley Reforms Act was passed. The period also witnessed the birth of new sprit among the people to fight against British rule and in course of it undergoes any sacrifice so long as that then took nearer to their goal.

After this many resolutions were passed in 1917 and 1919 for attaining the self-rule and swaraj. Consequently, next major development was drafting by Mrs. Annie Basant Common Wealth of India Bill of 1925. The Bill had demanded: (a) liberty of person and security of his dwelling and property; (b) freedom of conscience and free profess of religion; (c) free

54. Dr. K.K. Usman, This is Islam (1998), p. 47.
55. B.R. Sharma, Socio-Economic Justice under Indian Constitution, (1984), p. 36.
56. *Ibid.*

expression of opinion and right to assembly peaceably and without arm and forming association; (d) free elementary education; (e) use roads, public places, court of justice; (f) equality before law; and (g) equality of sex.[57]

The Nehru Committee Report of 1929 which resembled the Anne Basant Bill also included the list of rights.

The historical session of Lahore of which Jawaharlal Nehru was made President gave voice to new militant spirit and proceeds resolution of puran swaraj.[58] The Congress Resolution of 1924 also emphasized the theme of socio-economic reconstruction when it declared:

The poverty and misery of Indian people are due, not only to foreign exploitation in India but also due to the economic structure of the society, which the alien supports so that exploitation continues. In order to remove this poverty and misery and ameliorate the condition of Indian masses, it is essential to make revolutionary changes in present economic and social structure of society and to remove the gross inequalities.[59]

The Round Table Conference

After the Round Table Conference the British Government in March 1933 issues white paper outlining its proposal for constitutional reforms in India. But, this paper did not mention any type of socio-economic right. That is why this paper was condemned by all political parties and for the first time in the history of India Congress had demanded constituent assembly for framing Indian Constitution.

The subject of fundamental rights and its incorporation in the future Constitution of India was discussed at length by Sapru Committee in 1945 with Sir Tej Bahadur Sapru as its Chairman. It had issued questionnaire to various associations, groups and individuals soliciting their views on desirability of inclusion of fundamental rights.

---

57. Sudesh Kamar Sharma, Directive Principles and Fundamental Rights (1999), p. 137.
58. B.R. Sharma, Socio-Economic Justice under Indian Constitution, (1984), p. 41.
59. *Id.*, p. 41.

Finally Sapru Committee came on conclusion that fundamental rights should be justiciable and directive principles non-justiciable. These provisions were taken by Sapru Committee from Irish Constitution.[60] On the other hand, various Indian leaders have contributed to give social, economic, political justice in our Constitution. For example, contribution of Mahatma Gandhi, Pandit Jawaharlal Nehru, and Dr. B.R. Ambedkar cannot be forgotten. There is need to brief introduction of their concept of social justice.

Pandit Nehru's Vision of Social Justice

Nehru was a statesman and represented the orientive impulse of modern India.

Constitution of Pt. Nehru in the making of Constitution cannot be limited within words. He has given soul to the Constitution of India. In Constitution of India various provisions which deal with social justice have been incorporated on the lines of Nehru's thoughts. He has written in his autobiography that "our final aim can only be a classless society with equal economic justice and opportunity for all, a society organized on planned basis for raising mankind to higher material and cultural level to cultivation of spiritual values of cooperation unselfishness, the spirit of service, the desire to do light, goodwill and live ultimately a moral order."

Pandit Jawaharlal Nehru wanted to eradicate all types of discrimination. He was follower of socialism. He then explained objectives of socialism in following words:

> Our ideal is that every man, woman and child in India should have equal opportunities and that big disparities should go.[61]

Nehru believed that every body is born free and equal and capable of having right. He condemned discrimination based on race, religion, cast, sex and language as irrational because in all these situations person's free choice is not involved.

60. *Id.* p. 42.
61. *Id.* p. 90.

Gandhian Concept of Social Justice

Gandhian concept of social justice cannot be confined in few words on the paper. Contribution of Mahatma Gandhi in the freedom struggle and of nation building cannot be forgotten. He was not great because he liberated India from the British colonialism, but he was great for he suffered for suffering people.[62]

His compassion for people was not confined within the India but to the whole people of the world. Throughout his life he concentrated his entire attention for the upliftment of the weakest man of society and always explored avenues for welfare of such people.

Gandhian concept of social justice is based on the removal of all artificial inequalities among the human beings. No person is born untouchable and unequal. Removal of untouchability means removal of social barriers and inequalities.[63] He wanted to abolish all types of inequalities including economic. That is why Gandhiji talks about village economy and concept of self-reliance. According to Gandhiji men are born equal in the sense that they have right to equal opportunities. It can be said in brief that Gandhian concept of social justice is based on the principal that each should get according to his ability and each according to need. Equality, justice are based on concept of social justice as Gandhiji said. Adlous Huxley, about the Gandhiji's concept of social justice writes that, Gandhi's economic idea is based upon a realistic appraisal of man's nature and the nature of position of the universe. He did not accept economy as only a national standard of living of the individual, but as a means to establish higher social values. Such an economical system should not go against self-interest of any individual.[64]

Self-reliance, truth, non-violence, is main pillars of Gandhian philosophy. Gandhiji had totally humanitarian approach towards human beings. Nobody is above the human values and nobody shall make discrimination on the basis of

62. Rattan Das, The Global Vision of Mahatma Gandhi, (2005), p. 135.
63. S.H. Patil, Gandhi and Swaraj, (1983), p. 58.
64. Rattan Das, The Global Vision of Mahatma Gandhi, (2005), p. 146.

religion, caste, place of birth. His concept of social justice means everybody is equal and treated equally. Explaining Swaraj of his dream Gandhiji said :

> The Swaraj of my/our dream recognize no race or redefinitions. Not it is to be the monopoly of lettered persons, not yet of men and men. Swaraj is to be for all including the former, but emphatically including the maimed and blind, the staring, toiling million, a stout hearted honest, sane illiterate man may well be first servant of the nation.

Dr. B.R. Ambedkar's View on Social Justice

Dr. B.S. Ambedkar is called the father of the Constitution of India. He always laid the stress on the upliftment of lower castes. He wanted equality or a society where everybody is equal and treated equally. The sensitive jurist late Justice Gajendragadkar long ago, paid homage to Ambedkar's principle of social equality.

Some time, I feel that economic reform may not be completely successful unless social equality is established. The result of national concentration on political freedom without realizing that political freedom must involve social equality and economic justice has been that our social structure today remains substantially what it was before were attained political freedom and that is matter which ought to cause the gravest concern all sensitive and sensible men and women in our country.[65]

Ambedkar was of the opinion that these lower classes should be economically strong only then social justice can be possible in society.

With the efforts of Dr. Bhim Rao Ambedkar reservation provisions were added in our Constitution. In the beginning these provisions were made for only ten years, but ten years time was not felt adequate to eradicate this inequality because these classes are victim of many centuries.

65. V.R. Krishna Iyer, Dr. Ambedkar and the Dalit Future, (1990), p. 30.

It can be said concretely that social justice in view of Ambedkar meant to provide social, economic, political equality to these downtrodden classes.

Constitution of India and Concept of Social Justice

It was on the fateful mid-night of 14th August, 1947 at Zero hour that we attained freedom from foreign rule. We did so through our own efforts, guided by dedicated persistent leadership and the united efforts and sacrifices of our people. Hence, the major task before the country at that time was to outline the pattern of society for the future, keeping in view past traditions and providing ample opportunities for people to develop fast to catch up with the more progressive and advanced nations. The abundant resources of the country, both human and natural, were to be explored, developed and utilized. India, therefore, declared its policy of the Welfare State. As such on November 21, 1949 the Constitution of India was adopted with a resolution to constitute India into a Sovereign Democratic Republic and to secure to its entire citizen, social, economic and political justice with equality of status and opportunity. As foundation of democratic ideals, it guaranteed the citizens certain fundamental right to progress towards the goal of social justice and equality, the opportunity was to be facilitated by the directive principles of state policy.[66]

The concept of social justice, economic justice and political justice is living concept of the Constitution of India.

The Concept of Fundamental Rights

Fundamental rights are incorporated of Indian Constitution. The fundamental rights are necessary consequence of declaration in the Preamble to the Constitution that the people of India have solemnly resolved to constitute India into a sovereign, socialistic democratic republic and secure to all citizens justice social, economic and political and liberty of thought, expression belief, faith, worship and equality of status and opportunity.

The fundamental rights guaranteed certain economic rights. Too much emphasis on these rights might have led to

66. Dr. Gajendragadkar, Law, Society and Education, (1973), p. 1.

the emergence of a *laissez faire* economy in India now an out of date concept. Accordingly partly by judicial interpretation and partly by constitutional amendment process, emphasis has come to be laid on social control in economic matter leading to emergence of a regulated economy.[67]

The fundamental rights are fundamental because nobody develop himself without these rights and on the other hand they are justiciable in nature. Hence, it can be said that these rights are based on social, economic and political justice.

Directive Principles of State Policy

Directive Principles of State Policy are based on the concept of social good. They give direction to implement the certain policies which are laid down under the Constitution of India. These directive principles give stress on social justice.

Means of livelihood, distribute economic system, no concentration of wealth, equal pay for equal work, welfare of children, bandhua labour, free legal aid, village panchayat, social service, conditions of work, living wages, participation of workers in management of industries, uniform civil code, provisions for free and compulsory education, economic empowerment, raising standard of living,[68] all these are directive principles of state policy which give direction to the government to implement these principles for bringing justice-based society. But these principles are non-justiciable in nature.

2.9 PLANNING AND SOCIAL JUSTICE

When India got freedom in 1947, Pandit Jawaharlal Nehru adopted mixed economy where capitalistic or socialism goes parallel. India also adopted five year plans which were based on Russian Economic Development. In planning, government has from time to time given stress on social justice.

Objectives of Second Five Year Plan were to reduce the inequalities in income and wealth and more even distribution of economic power.[69]

67. M.P. Jain, Indian Constitutional Law, (2003), p. 974.
68. *Id.*, p. 1629.
69. K.C. Gopalakrishna, Legal Economic International Dimensions of Economic and Law, (1998), p. 299.

The objective of the Third Five Year Plan were broadly the same as in second plan but one more objective was added, i.e. achievement of self-sufficiency in food grain and increase in agricultural production to meet the requirement of industry and export.[70]

The main emphasis in the Fifth Five Year Plan was on 'garibi hatao' and 'self-reliance' to achieve the social justice. The main features of the Fifth Five Year Plan were :

(i) Promoting the active involvement of all sections of the people in the process of development through appropriate education, communication and institutional strategies.
(ii) Progressive reduction in regional inequalities.
(iii) Strengthening the impulse in modernization for achievement of economic and technical self-reliance.[71]

In the Seventh Five Year Plan emphasis had been given to the development of women and children and other vulnerable groups, creating facilities for universalization of elementary education and eradication of illiteracy in working age population and bringing down the population below the poverty line.[72]

The objective of social justice as laid down in these plans has many dimensions to improve the living standard of the poorest people, to remove poverty and unemployment and reduction in inequalities of income and wealth. All these aspects are mutually inclusive. To achieve social justice, a number of poverty alleviation and employment generation programmes have been launched. First of all Integrated Rural Development Plan, which aims at improving the lots of the rural poor consisting of landless labour, small marginal farmers, rural artisans. To support IRDP two sub-programmes of training of rural youth for self-employment and

70. Government of India, Third Five Year Plan.
71. K.C. Gopalakrishna, Legal Economic International Dimensions of Economic and Law, (1998), p. 30.
72. *Ibid.*, p. 30.

development of women and children in rural areas have also been launched.

The second category includes special area development programme such as Drought Prone Area Programme and Drought Programme which aim at optimum utilization of land, water, livestock, farm, forestry, diary development and development of subsidiary occupation in drought prone and desert area to raise the income of weaker sections of the society.

Third category included such employment generation programme such as National Rural Development Programme, Rural Landless Employment Guarantee Programme[73] which aims at creating supplementary employment opportunities during lean employment periods of the year. For more effective implementation of wage employment programmes NREP, RLEGP have been merged into Jawahar Rozgar Yojana since 1989. The emphasis has shifted toward rural works and works relating to land development to provide continue benefit to members of poverty groups. Fourth, there is minimum need programme which aims at improving the consumption level of the poorer section in order to raise their productive efficiency. Lastly, the other measures for achieving social justice have been land reforms, abolition of bounded labour, liquidation of rural indebtness, fixation of minimum wages for farm labour, etc.

2.10 LAND REFORMS AND CONCEPT OF SOCIAL JUSTICE

Indian economy is agricultural-based economy. More than 65 percent population depends on agriculture for their livelihood. In that situation land reforms are necessary for economic development or growth. The Constitution of India under Article 39(b)(c) talks about economic reform. Article 39(b) says that ownership and control of material resources of the community are to be so distributed as best to sub-serve the common good and Article 39(c) further says that the operation

73. M.L. Jihigan, The Economics of Development and Planning, 23rd ed., p. 903.

of the economic system does not result in the concentration of wealth and means of production to the common detriment.

On the other hand, the Planning Commission has also realized the importance of land reforms for the economic development of India. Therefore, government has undertaken several measures of land reforms in India for economic development. In Japan Meji (era 1879-1911)[74] reforms have occurred and in the similar manner in 1927 Russia has made collective reform and in the China under the slogan of the 'land to the tiller' various land reforms have been introduced. Taking example from these countries Indian government adopted the polities for land reforms. Main cause of land reform is that our biggest part of Gross Domestic Product (GDP) comes from the agriculture. Then only land reform can provide stability in the economic development of the country. This is why government has made different land reforms for making economic development table and durable.

2.11 NEW ECONOMIC POLICY AND SOCIAL JUSTICE

> "There is only one thing in this world, and that is to keep acquiring money and more money, power and more power. All the rest is meaningless."[75]

Economic reforms introduced in 1991 by the Congress government led by P.V. Narasimha Rao have completed thirteen years. The period is long enough to make an assessment of their impact on the common man in terms of more employment stabilization and price of articles of essential consumption or control of inflation, a better spread of growth benefiting the weaker section of the society—in other words, its effect on social justice. From the middle of 90 there was increased criticism that economic reform was *adhoc* and not driven by clear goal and objectives.[76]

---

74. M.L. Jihigan, The Economics of Development and Planning, 23rd ed., p. 903.
75. K.C. Gopalakrishna, Legal Economic International Dimensions of Economic and Law, (1998), p. 318.
76. Justice V.R. Krishna Iyer, "Legally Speaking", ed. 2004, p. 97.

After 1991 we have adopted the globalize economy that is why we are in midst of two mega trends:

(1) Globalization of the economy.
(2) Revival of the market with privatization as focal point.

There are four dimensions of globalization :

(1) National State System
(2) World capitalist economy
(3) World military order
(4) International division of labour

All are four interact with each other and influence the globalization process.[77] India also adopted this economic system after 1991 but this policy started their effect on the concept of social justice. If we start the effect of new economic policy then we come on the conclusion that it also affects poverty employment agriculture form, social security.

Economic Reform and their Impact on Poverty

A recent study shows that rural poverty declined from 31.6 percent in 1993-94 to 28.8 in 1999-2000 and urban poverty decline only by 6.5 percent during 1993-2000. Differences among various studies on decline in poverty range from the official 10 percent to 3 percent during the period 1993-2000.

The rate of decline for schedule caste living below poverty line was marginally lighter that of total population and the schedule caste also decreased during the same period in both urban and rural area. However, poverty among the schedule caste still continues very high with 38 percent in the rural and 37.84 percent in urban area. Similarly, poverty among scheduled tribes also decline along with general population. But incidence of poverty among schedule tribes continues to high with 45.86 percent and 34.74 percent living below the poverty line in rural and urban area.[78]

77. Economic Reforms since 1991 (IGNOU School of Management), p. 97.
78. K.C. Gopalakrishnan, "Legal Economics", ed. 1998, p. 425.

Economic Reforms and Employment

The present rising unemployment is primarily an outcome of a declining job-creating capacity of growth observed since 1993-94. The employment growth fell to 1.07 percent per annum between (1993-2000) from 2.7 percent per annum in pre-reform period (1983-94) in spite of acceleration in GDP growth from 5.2 percent to 6.7 percent between 1993-94 to 1999-2000. It means that capacity of job creation per unit of out went down abut three time captured to that in early so as early 90.[79]

Economic Reform and Agriculture

Agriculture is the way of life in Indian society. But after 1991 investment in agriculture is low down growth in agriculture. GDP declined from 3.4 percent in the 1980, 3 percent in the 1990. In the post liberalization period it declined from 4.7 percent in the Eighth Plan period to 1.8 percent in the Ninth Plan period. Due to revival of monsoon agriculture during the second quarter of 2003-04 was 7.4 percent. The expected growth rate was high due to pleasant monsoon. After 1991 Indian has adopted the new economic policy for bring the high growth rate but this policy effect the social justice very deeply. Particular working class is affected by this policy. This policy has created the great dialectic between directive principles of state policy. The biosphere is not being bashed by Multi-national Companies which have nobody to be burnt nor soul to be demanded as Maneka Gandhi once said :

> "Our government thinks that the unemployment problem in the country will get solved when these multinationals set-up a number of industries here. The fact is, they are not going to set-up the labour-oriented industries in first place to solve the unemployment problem; secondly, they are not interested in setting up their factories in under-developed area. The third and most important danger is they are coming out with those projects which are banned in their countries for environmental reason. In effect, we

79. Economic Reforms since 1991, (IGNOU School of Management), p. 102.

> are giving red carpet welcome to those industries which have banned in the developed countries. They will pollute the entire atmosphere and we will be compelled to drink polluted water and breathe polluted air. If these indiscriminate sanctions for environmentally hazardous industry continue, India will be doomed forever; we cannot allow that to happen.[80]

In this demystifying criticism aimed at the social justice claptrap popular in capitalist. Milieu of our judicial jurisprudent who attack the fringes with bursts of rhetoric but retreat artfully where the basic capitalistic structure may fracture. In short, social justice embroidery or cardiac surgery in the system which flourishes on profit for corporate privateers dismissing man as but the tail end of a tube warm.[81] Justice Iyer says in such capitalistic pattern of society you cannot expect social justice. In capitalistic pattern of society you cannot expect the socialism.

The modern scientific advance of civilization becomes a victim of venality, vulgarity, violence, voluptuous violation of morality and pathological displacement of finer values by brutal torture and outrageous terrorism. It is a lunatic catastrophe, the world over, inspite of materialistic science and fantastic technology, marvel and medieval discovery and extra ordinary exploration of out space. Developed society has become a savage menagerie, wise man has cost their voice and weight and money dominates man and his faculties. Divinity has been suppressed by barbarity, social justice by capitalistic greed and malignant megalomania imperialist arrogance and heartless adventurism of big powers has eclipsed the united nation. International law is now on the vanishing point of jurisprudence. Aggressive industrialization and commercialized agriculture are a racketeering operation against nature. Even education and public health governed by market forces and commodities of high prices.[82]

80. Economic Reforms since 1991 (IGNOU School of Management), p. 102.
81. Justice V.R. Krishna Iyer, "Legally Speaking", ed. 2004, p. 97.
82. Justice V.R. Krishna Iyer, "Social Justice Sun Set and Dawn, ed. 1987, p. 2.

In era of privatization and globalization is responsible for negation of equal opportunity, social justice and suppression of dignity and access to education. Triple capitalistic mantra of globalization, liberalization and privatization. India had its own world stature but the kremlin having committed defacto harakri, non-align movement having vanished its importance. Manmohanmics, which is applied ragenomices come to say and dependencia syndrome subtly sabotaged Swaraj, Swedeshi and Socialism.[83] Iyer criticize new economic policy and said that some corporate arrive in India with hunger for profit. Iyer is of the opinion that new economic policy is against Part III, IV, and IVA of Indian Constitution. Iyer said that our finance minister whichever party in power, have gone for General Agreement on Tariffs and Trade, Trade Relating Intellectual Properties. World Trade Organization which is loyal to America incorporated. Although India is governed by the socialistic secular democratic Constitution, an objective student of politics and economics will sadly reflect on the somber reality that dominating foreign investment has free to exploit India.[84] Iyer says that these all policies are against constitutional philosophy and we cannot expect social justice in era of globalization, privatization or liberalization. That is why he said that we should not change our constitutional jurisprudence by making copy of west intoxicated economy. Our socio-economic conditions are different from those countries. Social justice enshrined in our Constitution we cannot ignore the provision of Constitution which based on social revolution. Iyer says that by these policies we supported capitalistic economy where money is everything. Moreover, our constitution start with great five worlds, We the People of India. In brief it can be said that this policy is against social justice.

The basic features of our Constitution include the rule of law, the socialistic pattern of economy implied in social justice and egalitarian ethos supremacy of Parliament, final authority of Supreme Court on law, subject of sovereignty of We the people of India. The Indian republic itself is explicitly socialist

83. Justice V.R. Krishna Iyer, "Judges Postpouri", ed. 2007, p. 12.
84. Conference Organised by I.A.L. in Chandigarh in February 2007.

and democratic, whoever be allergic, new economic policy, new industrial policy, new declaration of liberalization, privatization permissiveness towards monopolies exploitation, friendly invitation for foreign capital and multinationals. In the end, Justice Iyer said that:

> "Every gun that is made, every warship launched, every rocket fired signifies in the final sense a theft from those who hunger and are not fed, those who are called and are not clothed. This world is arms are not spending money alone, it is spending the sweat of its labourer's the genius of its scientists, the hopes of its children.

Today Indian society is in the third stage of economic development. It slowly and steadily is moving towards an industrial society. After 1991 India had adopted economic liberalization for economic development of the country.

There is latent violation of labour laws and social justice has become victim. One thing should be clear that our Constitution is based on our culture and tradition, but when we interpret our Constitution we follow foreign and comparative jurisprudence, though our socio-economic conditions are different from those countries. There is need for human jurisprudence while making the law or while interpreting law or while we make economic policy for India.[85]

Economy is the base of all social life in the present society. We cannot deny this fact. No doubt our Constitution is good and based on the humanitarian jurisprudence but there is need to give practical implementation to these provisions only then social justice and economic justice is possible in the society.

---

85. Subrata Mukerjee, Sushila Ramaswamy, Great Western Political Thinkers, Deep & Deep Publications Pvt. Ltd., ed. 1998, p. 15.

3

Dimension of Social Justice

Iyer's Views

INTRODUCTION

Justice in the Indian context must be people-oriented. The vast majorities of people are poor, socially suppressed, and illiterate and steeped in rural backwardness. Any justice reform package must cognize the people factor, their village base, the feudal pyramid and urban extortion. The constitution has injected the spirit of rights, revolution and equal justice. So class justice is a lost cause in the long-run under upper berth justicing art must be given a long holiday. Human right postulates the right to life, to human dignity, to creative comforts, to cultural personhood for everyone.[1]

The main object of Justice delivery system is to satisfy the maximum wants of the human body. Subject matter of justice should be maximum happiness of common man. That is why Justice V.R. Krishna Iyer has said that we the people are touch

1. Justice V.R. Krishna Iyer, A Random Miscellany Legal and Other (1984), p. 15.

stone and whet stone, salus populi is suprema lax. Therefore, we must accept as an axiom of a progressive order that republic will run on the rails of the rule of law only through universal legal access to social justice.[2] If we study Indian Constitution we find that the whole Constitution of India is based on the concept of social justice. Justice Iyer has rightly said that social justice is the signature tune of Indian Constitution. When we speak of social justice in the Indian context we have to focus on its humane dynamics. We must sift the grain from the chaff and hierarchical justice from Egalitarian by the Doctrine of classification and Exclusion of steps for Equalization from the concept of Equality as devices for preservation of hierarchical *status quo* against the ideological assault of militant egalitarianism, breaking faith with midnight tryst. The content of social justice was best expressed in say eloquence by Nehru at the drawn of our freedom.

> The service of India means the service of millions who suffers. It means the ending of poverty and ignorance and disease and inequality of opportunity. The ambition of the greatest man of our generation has been to wipe every tear from every eye. That may be beyond us, but as long as there are tears and suffering, so long our work will not be over.[3]

Broad equality is also a crucial component of social justice. Even a total non-Marxist like Mathew Arnold has stated, thus: A society of unequal materializes our upper class, vulgarizes our middle class and brutalize our lower class.

To bring social justice in Indian society Indian Constitution has given Directive Principe of State policy and Fundamental Rights to Indian Society. These provisions have assigned the duty on central and state government to make such type of social order which is based on just and fair system. These fundamental rights and directive principles are

2. Justice V.R. Krishna Iyer, Some Half Hidden Aspect of Social Justice, (1979), p. 89.
3. *Ibid.*, p. 31.

conscience of Indian Constitution. But Justice V.R. Krishna Iyer criticizes the government for the non-implementation of Directive Principles and ignoring the fundamental rights while pressing his anguish and anger, he quotes Bernard Shaw:

> "I, am and have always been and shall now always be a revolutionary writer, because our laws make law impossible; our liberties destroy all freedom; our property is organized robbery; our morality is an impudent hypocrisy; our wisdom is administrated by inexperience or male experiences, dupes our power wielded by cowards and weaklings, and our honour false in all its points. I am an enemy of the existing order".[4]

Krishna Iyer wants to synthesize the Directive Principles and Fundamental Rights, before giving social justice there must be economic justice as envisaged by the Directive Principles. That is why in most of his judgments he stressed the need to implement Directive Principles of State Policy.

In Iyer's views social justice is a generous concept which assures to every member of society fair deal. Any remedial injury, injustice, inadequacy or disability suffered by a member for whom he is not directly responsible falls within the liberal connotation of social justice.[5]

Justice Iyer agrees with Nehru and olds that socialism is the aim of our Constitution. Justice Iyer believes that maximization of collective resources of community, natural and human and their equitable distribution, each getting according to his need is social justice in its productive and distributive facets. He emphasizes that:

> "Social justice is struggling to be born and constitutional organ must mid-wife it".[6]

Justice Iyer divides justice in different forms, for example, social justice, political justice, economic justice, distributive

4. *Supra* note 1, p. 61.
5. See, Shilja Chander, Justice V.R. Krishna Iyer on Fundamental Rights and Directive Principles, (1998), p. 10.
6. *Ibid.*, p. 17.

justice. Under the concept of social justice, justice Iyer gives stress on socialistic pattern of society. According to Iyer in capitalism competition, business, contract you cannot expect social justice. Iyer is of the opinion that production is base of society and human beings. Social justice is only possible when there is equal distribution of economic resources among the human beings, and only then equal participation can be ensured in all spheres of human life.

To sum up in the words of Daniel Webster, whose ideals are closer to Krishna Iyer?

> Justice is the greatest interest of man on earth. It is the ligament which holds civilized being's and civilized national together. Justice is end of government. It is the end of the civil society. It behooves us therefore, to bring into fruition justice which is truth in action and make the legal system in each country viable as an instrument of national fulfilment.[7]

3.1 CLASSIFICATION OF JUSTICE ACCORDING TO JUSTICE V.R. KRISHNA IYER

Justice Iyer, who is a strong supporter of social justice, classifies justice in different forms:

(1) Economic justice
(2) Political justice
(3) Industrial justice
(4) Judicial justice
(5) Distributive justice
(6) Constitutional Justice

Economic Justice

Economic justice of individual level means the legitimate proceeds of his labour. To work according to ability and get according to need seems yet to be a distant goal, work seems yet to be a distant goal, work whether mental or manual to be basically assigned to economic justice is to ensure that one

7. *Ibid.*, pp. 23-24.

who put in any labour must take the desert of his labour.[8] But Iyer's views on Economic justice mean curtail the eternal conflict between capital and labour. Equal wages for equal work is the foremost condition of labour force. Article 39(d) of the Constitution direct the state policy towards securing equal pay for equal work and maternity relief. Article 43 mandates participation of worker in the management of industry.

Economic justice deals with distribution of Economic Resources. Iyer is of the opinion that production is the basics of all social life and economic justice is based on solid concept of distribution of economic resources among common man of the society. Only then economic justice is helpful for providing social justice. Iyer said that economic developments that have taken place in the country cannot be denied. The unfortunate thing is that this is no just sharing of developments. The fruits of economic progress instead of being shared by masses flow into the pockets of the traders, businessman and industrialists. Even the civil servants and active politicians are taking undue advantage of their position and delivering the shares of the masses towards their own relative's trends and stooges. Again it is still more tragic that in socialist economy the price of food stuffs and essential consumer goods are soaring sky high. Failure of the government to control the price is in the ultimate analyses denial of economic justice.[9]

When Gandhiji gave a call for economic justice to him economic justice meant that every one should be free from want of food, clothing and shelter. Everyone should get the basic necessaries of life.[10] But when India got the freedom we adopted Directive Principles of State policy and our constitution maker had the vision of socialism. Under socialism, there is need for equitable distribution of means of production and other resources. But our governments have adopted the mixed economy where private and public sector go together. But, on the other hand, economic justice demands the equal distribution of the means of production. Today,

8. Chaturvedi, Natural Social Economic Political Justice, (1990), p. 707.
9. Raj Bahadur Shrivastava, Economic Justice under Indian Constitution, (1989), pp. 31-32.
10. *Ibid.*, p. 20.

Indian economy is going towards the privatization where the rich become richer and poor become poorer. In that circumstances social justice remains on the paper and preamble promise: economic justice is only possible when every person is secure about his food, housing and decent standard of living.

Justice Iyer is of the opinion that social justice is only possible when there is economic justice in the society economic justice demands that there should equal distribution of means of production which in other words, means that there should be public ownership only then economic justice is possible.

Economic justice is essential component of social justice. Without economic justice social justice is mere mockery. Economic justice mean abolished eternal conflict between labour and capital. Under the Constitution of India, Directive Principle deals with economic justice and distribution of ownership among people. For production, workman and capital both are necessary to each other. Development does not start with goods. It starts with people and their education, organization and discipline without these three all resources remain talent, untapped potential.

Industrial jurisprudence must produce a comprehensive and effective code of industrial relation and regulation expressing social philosophy of the Constitution which is not aligned.[11]

We are socialist Republic and social justice is signature tune of our Constitution, we are hungry and poor and need all resources even to survive.

In Industrial jurisprudence relationship of master-servant or in modern terminology the relationship between employer and employee originated in that contract and started with scepter of hire and fire after the eclipse of paternalistic system of domestic economy on account of the industrial revolution.[12]

Labour economics examines the organization, uniting and outcomes of labour markets. The decision of prospective and present labour market participation, and the public policy

11. Justice V.R. Krishna Iyer, A Random Miscellany Legal and Other, (1981), p. 7.
12. Johari, S.N., Industrial Jurisprudence, (1984), p. 9.

relating to the employment and payment of labour resources.[13] Labour economics or industrial jurisprudence demand that there should be balance of interest between employer and employee. Labour is important component of production. Justice V.R. Krishna Iyer also demands common ownership of industry and means of production.

Welfare and social order is industrial settings depend on productivity, development and modern technique, forces of labour market, degree of effective organization of worker as trade union and the employer association.[14] The main function of labour law is to make balance between interest of labour and industrialist. Justice V.R. Krishna Iyer was in favour of minimum wages. Labour law curtails conflict between capital and labour. But today in era of capitalism, globalization or privatization, labour as become commodity of production. In such system worker has been paid for capacity of work. But Justice V.R. Krishna Iyer has widen the dimension of Industrial Jurisprudence and Industrial Justice at large sense.

Political Justice

The subject matter of political justice is the reasonableness entering within the enjoy ability of and the impossibility of restriction on fundamental rights meaning thereby political justice is the balance between the rights and their restrictions which is same thing as balance between the individual and the state which is a different thing, from the balance between two conflicting rights of two particular individuals or group of individuals.[15] Political justice is life of democracy; it makes the balance between individual and state rights and also put the reasonable restriction, over ruler and citizen. Political justice ensures a system of free and fair elections participated by one and all, without discrimination on grounds of religion, race, caste sex, or any of them, a system known as universal adult suffrage. But V.R. Krishna Iyer says that political justice in India has starting losing its existence. "have not's are rapidly

13. Compbell, Slanlay, David, Contemporary Labour Economic, (1999), p. 1.
14. Johri, S.N., Industrial Jurisprudence, (1984), p. 34.
15. *Supra* n. at p. 640.

losing faith in the representative pretence of popular government. The millions of people who make up the weaker section have no voice or space in state power. Through mega propaganda, .political pressure and mafia-operated minimal votes, they rule the State and run its instrumentalities. This is not government by the people our colossal system is extravagantly expensive. It alienated the indigent and the backward from candidature or choice of candidates or decisive voting influence. The democratic drapery of our Constitution stands shrunken with commitment to Swaraj, national unity and patriotic fraternity eclipsed. What prevails is tycoon Raj and foreign investment craze, five star stylelife style addition captured by west intoxicated culture of the exploitative creamy layer with a capitalist kink.[16]

Industrial Justice

Justice Iyer also talks about industrial justice. Indeed the concept of social justice has now become such part of industrial law that it would be ideal for any party to suggest that industrial adjudication can or should ignore claims of social justice in dealing with industrial disputes. The concept of social justice is not narrow, or one sided or pedantic and is not confined to industrial adjudication alone.[17] Its sweep is comprehensive. It is founded on the basic ideal of socio-economic equality and its aim is to assist the removal of social economic disparities and inequalities.[18]

Industrial justice occupies an important place in the industrial society. Iyer concept of industrial justice is to curtail the gap between labour and capital. At international level there is international labour organization which deals with industrial justice. All men are equal, are created equal. The principle of equality and non-discrimination has been internationally recognized as back as 1919 when the preamble of international labour organization provided for principle of equal remuneration for work of equal value for this first time.

16. V.R. Krishna Iyer, Democracy and Election Process, *The Hindu*, Wednesday, 4 July, 2007.
17. By P.G. Krishna, Economic Justice and the Indian Constitution: Some Implication of Bonus Case, *JILI*, (1966), Vol. 8, p. 458.
18. *Ibid.*, 458.

The Philadelphia Declaration of 1944 proclaimed that all human beings, irrespective of race, creed or sex have the right to produce both their material well-being and spiritual development in condition of freedom, dignity, economic security and equal opportunity.[19]

That is why Iyer speaks about industrial jurisprudence and stresses the need to implement the conventions of international labour organization. He has said that industrial jurisprudence must produce a comprehensive and effective code of industrial relation and regulation expressing the social philosophy of Constitution. Industrial justice is only possible when worker participate in the management of industry and get the living wages. The concept of social justice has become integral part of industrial law. In the industrial set-up social justice implies two things: first, an equitable distribution of profit and other benefits accruing from industry between owner of industry, say industrialist and worker and secondly, providing or affording protection to workers against harmful effect to their health, satisfy and morality.[20]

The workers and employer are the two pillars of our national economy. The relationship between worker and employer is one of partnership in the maintenance of production and say the building up of national economy.[21]

We cannot ignore the role of worker in increasing the productivity. In this connection upliftment of labour in social and economic spheres is necessary for industrial peace. Industrial justice demands that there should be balance of interest between employer and labour. In India, several legislations have been passed in this regard. These include: Workmen Compensation Act, 1923, Trade Union Act, 1926, Industrial Dispute Act, 1947, Minimum Wages Act, 1948, The Factory Act, 1948, Maternity Benefit Act, 1961, Payment of Bonus Act, 1965, Payment of Gratuity Act, 1972, Equal Remuneration Act, 1976, etc.

19. O.P. Parmar, ILO and India in Pursuit of Human Rights through Labour Standard, *JILI*, (1981), 555.
20. S.M. Chaturvedi, Labour and Industrial Law, (1995), 1.
21. *Ibid.*, 1.

All these acts are based on industrial justice and peace and seek to provide social security to the working class.

During his judgeship Justice V.R. Krishna Iyer has delivered some modest judgments regarding Industrial Jurisprudence. In *Statesman Ltd.* v. *Workmen,*[22] Justice Krishna Iyer observes that labour litigation can be curse ordered where one side is weak, and has not been able to hire legal services but has been made good by amicus curial. and other side, regardless the court is anxious to settle some principle as counsel for appellant impressed on us. We now move into area of facts which wears jural apparel.

At certain stages of conflict in this world face saving is more important than heart searching. Life is no logic and prestige amends propriety.[23]

In *Mumbai Kamgar Sabha* v. *Abdul Bhai,*[24] Justice Krishna Iyer points out that organized labour inevitably involves unionization welfare of workers being a primary concern of our Constitution. Since we are not called upon investigation the veracity of claim we stop with stating that employer's awareness of social justice which fertilizer the right of his employee for bonus. All this is indirect bonanza of part IV of the Constitution of India which bespeaks the conscience of nation including the community of employees. Law is not petrified by the past, but response to call of the changing time. So too the social consciousness of employee labour has its legal moral duty to the community for an undisciplined contribution to the health and wealth of industry. Law is not always an organizer of one way traffic.

Today it is accepted doctrine; labour is the backbone of the nation, particularly in area of economic self-reliance. This means the welfare of working classes is not only a human problem but a case where success of the nation's economic adventure depends on cooperation of working class to make better India. Every law consists of two parts—body and soul. The letter of law is body of the law, and sense and reason of law is the soul of law.[25]

22. AIR 1976 SC 758.
23. *Id.*
24. AIR 1976 SC 1455.
25. AIR 1976 SC 1455.

In *Rohtas Industries* v. *Rohtas Industries Staff Union,*[26] Justice Krishna Iyer points out that the legislative and judicial process have promise to keep its positive industrial pace in tune with distributive and economic justice and continuity of active production were to accomplished.

In *Straw Board Management* v. *Its Workmen,*[27] Justice Krishna Iyer says that life of right is remedies and jurisprudence of ready relief alone can inhibit the weaker numbers of our land. Judges occupies the public bench of justice. They implement the public sense of justice. If the court is fulcrum of the justice system, there is strong case for the reform of court methodology and bestowal of attention of efficient management of judicial administration. Industrial jurisprudence demands balance between capital and labour. Law especially labour law is the art of economic order sustained by social justice. It aims at pragmatic, success but is guided by realities. We should guided by realistic judicial responses to societal problems against the back drop of the new radial values implied in social justice to labour. The production backbone of the nation adjusted to environs of the particular industry and its economics.

The recent constitutional amendment (Article 43A) which emphasis the worker role in production as partners in process read in the light of the earlier accent on worker rights and social justice, gives a news status and sensitivity to industrial jurisprudence in our socialistic Republic.

Referring Cardozo's, "The Nature of the Judicial Process" Justice Krishna Iyer quoted:

> "That court best serves the law which recognizes that the rules of law which grew up on a remote generation may, in the fullness of experience, be found of serve another generation badly, and which discards the old rule when it finds that another rule of law represents what should be according to the established and settled judgment of society, and no considerable property rights have become vested in reliance upon the old rule.

26. AIR 1976 SC 425.
27. AIR 1977 SC 941.

In *Bangalore Water Supply* v. *A. Rajappa*,[28] Justice Krishna Iyer observed that, likewise an industry cannot exist without cooperative endeavour between employer and employee. No employer and employee, no industry not as dogmatic proposition in economics but as an articulate major promise of the definition and scheme of Act.

In B. *Benerjee* v. *Anita*,[29] Justice Krishna Iyer says that, Law is a social science and constitutionality turns not on abstract principles or rigid legal canons but concrete realities and given conditions : for the rule of law stems from the rule of life. We emphasize this facet of sociological jurisprudence. Judges act not by hunch but on hard facts properly brought on record and sufficiently strong to rebuff the initial presumption of constitionality of legislation.

Justice Krishna Iyer further observes that the law is made for the bulk of the community to produce social justice and isolated instances of unintended injury are inevitable martyrs for the common good since God Himself has failed to make perfect laws and perfect justice.

There are some of the important judgments of Justice V.R. Krishna Iyer regarding the industrial jurisprudence and labuor economics. By these judgments we can assume that justice V.R. Krishna Iyer always favoured the labour class. He believed in a concept of each according to his need and each according to his ability. He want to abolish the eternal conflict between capital and labour and wanted to provide economic justice. There is nothing wrong if we say that justice Iyer is father of progressive industrial jurisprudence.

Judicial Justice

Iyer's concept of judicial justice deals with judicial process or functioning of legal system. In India though equal access to justice is guaranteed to all but when invoked by the poor it poses a plethora of hurdles that relegates the poor to resign his entitlements. Destitution, illiteracy, ignorance, social bondage and cultural inhibition seriously impair the accessibility of the poor, often resulting in total denial of

28. AIR 1977 SC 941.
29. AIR 1975 SC 1146.

justice. The primary requisite of judicial justice is common man's accessibility towards court or in other sense full opportunity to the common, down-trodden men to defend his claim. That is why Article 39A of Indian Constitution has been added in Indian Constitution by forty-second amendment, 1976. Article 39A enjoins the state to secure that the operation of the legal systems promotes justice, on the basis of equal opportunity and to provide free legal aid to ensure the opportunities for securing the justice.[30] Iyer is of the opinion that if the judicial process fails the people's sense of justice, violence fills the vacuums and the streets, not the courts, settle dispute.[31] For this judiciary should be fiduciary towards people. Judicial justice and social justice courts give man his due according law and social justice also demands to that every body would get his due. Judicial justice is instructional justice, much as the Supreme Court, various High Courts and the other subordinate courts. Judicial justice is part of social justice and social justice demands that when the man lives in the society he would get his due. That is why Iyer has said that it is duty of Judges, lawyers and police to help in administration of judicial justice, and then social justice is possible in the society. For judicial justice Iyer said that these should democratization of grass-root and even higher level judiciary. Equal justice under the law and the due process of law imply all this. The right of effective access to justice has emerged with new social right for judicial justice. There is need for democratization of court justice and full participation of common man in justice system. Iyer says that litigation is not fight between two wrestlers; it deals with common interest and emotion. It is the duty of the court to look after all the matter before giving decision. Judges are not monks and scientists; they are living being of the society. Therefore, judicial justice demands active role of judges in administration of justice in the common man's favour. It is duty of the judge to maintain confidence of common man towards courts otherwise people will take law in their hands. But for this judge has to play the dynamic role and only then we can

30. M. Hidaytullah, Constitutional Law of India, (1984), Vol. 1, p. 702.
31. V.R. Krishna Iyer, Courts on Trial, (1987), p. 17.

actualize the dream of social justice of our Constitution-maker. Iyer laments that our judicial system is colonial and based on imperialistic power. That is why he says that the consumer of this system are still the proprietariat, by and large, the common people being either anathema or allergic to the system.[32]

Distributive Justice

Distributive justice embraces the whole economic dimension of social justice, the entire question of proper distribution of goods and services within the society. It demands equality in the distribution or allotment of advantage or burden. Distributive justice aims to strike a balance in the socio-economic structure of the society to bring equalized between conflicting desires, interests and claims of individual citizen. Justice P.N. Bhagwati explains the distributive justice, "justice in depth, justice which penetrates and destroys inequalities of race, sex and wealth, justice which is not confined to a fortunate few, but takes within its sweep entire people of country, justice which ensures equitable distribution of social, material and political resources of the community".[33]

Justice V.R. Krishna Iyer speaks about distributive justice thus: special concern for backward human sector of the lowliest and the lost, and activist, affirmative state action for their advancement as democratic imperative, plus the organization of a sensitive and creative milieu which offer, as right, social economic cultural opportunity, dignity of personhood and individuality to every human, regardless of seeming or real disparities to unfold his full, mental, moral and physical potentional.[34]

Distributive justice, in the views of Krishna Iyer, means upliftment of the weaker section by giving special treatment to these people. Main object or subject of distributive justice makes balance of interest in the society. Distributive justice makes the three main pillars (i) to each according to his right,

32. V.R. Krishna Iyer, Our Courts on Trial (1987), p. 106.
33. Sudesh Kumar Sharma, Distributive Justice under Indian Constitution, (1989), p. 45.
34. *Ibid.*, p. 46.

(ii) to each according to his interest, and (iii) to each according to his need.

Protective discrimination and reservation policy are products of distributive justice. These policies are based on concept of distributive justice. Justice Iyer in *State of Kerala* v. *N.M. Thomas,* AIR 1976 SC 490 social engineering which the law in action must adopt new strategies to liquidate encrusted group injustices or surrender society to remain in tensions. Equilibrium in human terms emerges from releases of the handicapped and the primitive from persistent social disadvantage by determined creative and canny legal maneuvers of the State, not by hortative declaration positively in favour of weak may some times be promotion of genuine equality before the law".[35]

In this way justice Iyer has supported distributive justice. He scoffed at the law in its majestic equality where the rich and poor sleep under bridges to beg in the streets and steal bread. Redistributive justice to Harijan Community insists on effective reform, designed to produce equal partnership of the lowliest and the lost, by rude action informed by short-run and long-run sociologically potent perspective planning and implementation. An uneven socio-economic land scope hardly gives the joy of equal opportunity and development or draw forth their best from manpower resources how wallowing in the low visibility areas of disentangled life.[36]

Justice Iyer is a supporter of the reservation policy but he also said that it should not extend to the creamy layer but confirmed to common and down-trodden man. Only then we can expect the distributive justice or social justice from the policy.[37]

Iyer on Constitutional Justice

The jurisprudence woven around the preamble to our Constitution has many dimensions, radical and crimson. The value revolution and humanist transformation the Constitution has inaugurated, has yet to blossom fully to make the lives of

35. AIR (1976) SC 490.
36. AIR (1976), 490.
37. *Ibid.*

the many millions of our countrymen pulsate with material, moral and spiritual fulfilment. The great vision of our founding father was that a just social order should bloom into existence in the fullness of time where the lowliest, the lost and least among the near billion of Indian shall have fulfilment, not frustration, where the state shall strive to wipe every tear from every eye, where the people's sovereignty and democracy shall prevail.[38]

The Constitution is more than legal parchment. It is socio-economic instrument with a revolutionary thrust. Indeed the high purpose and the wealth of human right which inhere in the citizen of India by virtue of the Constitution are condensed with delicious brevity and precious dignity in the preambular passages. Indeed, we never forget people of India as whole, not the elite nor the up strata nor indeed, the power broker, but all the people are title holders under the Constitution.[39]

The one essential quality that distinguishes V.R. Krishna Iyer from his judicial brethren and puts him includes of his own is compassion.[40] Soli Sobrajee said that to my mind greatest contribution to our constitutional jurisprudence his landmark judgment in Samsher Singh which delivered under trying domestic circumstances on the account of his wife illness.[41]

Once Justice V.R. Krishna Iyer quoted following lines :

> I repeat—that all power is a trust—that we are accountable for its exercise that from the people, and for the people, all springs, and all must exist—Benjamin Disraeli,[42] Justice V.R. Krishna Iyer make the following quotation, "Parliament is not a congress of ambassadors from different and hostile interest : which interest each

38. Justice V.R. Krishna Iyer, "Human Rights Judge Miscellany, Pub. B.R. Publishing, Ed., 1995, pp. 29-30.
39. *Op. cit.*, p.30.
40. M.P.R. Nair, Justice Krishna Iyer at 90, Universal Publications, 2005, p. 50.
41. *Op. cit.*, p. 53.
42. Quoted in Justice V.R. Krishna Iyer, Judge's Postpouri, Universal Law Publishing, Ed., 2007, p. 10.

must maintain, as an Agency and advocate against the other advocates, but parliament is a deliberate assembly of one nation with one interest that of whole, not local purpose, not local prejudice right to guide, but the general good, revolting from the general reason of the whole."[43]

The Constitution in its preamble and fundamental right part has described the right to life with equality and social justice to every person who is a member of the grand collective, we the people of India as 'guaranteed right and paramount value.[44]

Indira Gandhi Asserted

To me, economic justice is an inseparable part of political freedom. Freedom is not freedom if it does not mean a better deal and more opportunity for the poor and the deprived.[45]

The basic features of our Constitution include the Rule of Law, the socialistic pattern of economy implied in social justice and equalitarian ethos, supremacy of parliament, final authority of the Supreme Court on Law, subject to the sovereignty of the We the People of India. The Indian Republic itself is explicitly socialist and democratic whoever be allergic.[46]

India has a cultural heritage of law and life. My thoughts spelt out above have a universal element and is India specific. Indeed, taking note of the evolving international legal order. Each systems must be related to its own background, taking full account of the historical agencies which have effected its genesis, with an eye, always upon the future.[47]

Mankind is one society containing many societies, each of which can contribute its own especial insights and draw upon

43. *Op. cit.*, p. 11.
44. *Op. cit.*, p. 15.
45. Justice V.R. Krishna Iyer, "Judge's Postpouri, Universal Law Publishing, Ed., 2007, p. 66.
46. *Op. cit.*, p. 67.
47. Justice V.R. Krishna Iyer, "Human Right—A Judge Miscellany, Ed., 1995, B.R. Publishing, p. 32.

its own especial experience in the development of rule of law within which legal aid is coming to be recognized as an inherent part.[48]

The principal aim of a socialist state to eliminate inequality in income and status and standards of life. The basic framework of socialism is to provide decent standard of life to the working people and especially provide security from cradle to grave. This amongst other on economic side envisaged economic equality and equitable distribution of income. This is a blend of Marxism and Gandhism leaving heavily towards Gandhian socialism. During the formative years socialism aims at providing all opportunities for pursuing the educational activity.[49]

When social justice becomes an end of government, liberation from privatization, nationalization and state ownership, distributive justice backed by the Rule of Law and various other salutary measures to make the right to life not a liability but a fulfilment becomes significant. While private enterprises is certainly permissible, the grantee of social justice to the people at large makes public control of the Nation Resources and stimulation of self-reliance to guard against erosion of sovereignty and other project and plans which make the republic truly independent becomes an imperative.[50]

3.2 DIRECTIVE PRINCIPLES AND SOCIAL JUSTICE

The relationship between directive principles of state policy and the fundamental rights has been subject matter of controversy since the commencement of the Constitution. Three different views have emerged regarding the interrelationship between two. One view maintains that fundamental rights are superior to directive principles of state policy and later must ran subsidiary to the former. This view is based on the quasi-natural law premise that there are certain rights which are paramount, immutable transcendental and are thus to so basic to the existence of the Constitution that they

48. *Op. cit.*, p. 34.
49. *Op. cit.*, p. 35.
50. *Op. cit.*, p. 41.

must prevail over any other part of the Constitution. This view also encapsulates the literal interpretation premise of the directive principle being not enforceable in a Court of law. The second view is that fundamental rights and directive principles are of equal efficacy and enjoy the equal place and significance in the constitutional set-up. The third view maintains that directive principles are superior to fundamental rights. This view is based on the stipulation contained in Article 37 that these principles are fundamental in the governance of the country and it shall be the duty of state to apply these principles.

Directive Principle of State Policy enshrines in Part IV of Indian Constitution further envisages the inclination of the Constitution-makers towards a socialistic state of the Indian Brand.[51] Our Constitution provides enough scope for socialistic pattern of society by giving place to these directive principles in Constitution. Although these directive principles has no judiciary protection but it is moral duty of administration to implement these principles because these are based on the concept of social good and social justice.

Before analyzing the content and spirit of the directive principles, it would be better to have a brief account of these principles. The first three Articles 36, 37 and 38, in this regard, are general in charter and deal with definition, legal effects and objectives. Rest of directive principles tests into three main categories : (1) Those that lead India towards welfare state or so-called socialistic pattern of state, (2) Principles based on Gandhian thoughts relating to social upliftment and village panchayats, and (3) The principles of relating to promotion of international peace and security.

These directive principles of state policy reveal social mission of Indian Constitution. Article 38 directs the state "to promote the welfare of the people of securing and protecting as effectively as it may a social order in which justice social economic and political shall inform of the institution of the national life.

51. Chandrika Singh, Constitutional Battle in India, (2001), p. 37.

Article 39 stipulates that the state shall, in particular, direct its policy towards securing:

(a) That the citizens, men and women equally, have the right to an adequate means of livelihood;
(b) The ownership and control of material resources of the community are so distributed as best to sub-serve the common good;
(c) That the operation of the economic system does not result in the concentration of wealth and means of production to the common detriment;
(d) That there is equal pay for equal work for both men and women;
(e) That the health and strength of workers, men and women and the tender age of children are not abused and that citizens are not forced by economic necessity to enter avocations unsuited to their age and strength; and
(f) That children are given opportunities and facilities to develop in a health manner and in conditions of freedom and dignity and that childhood and youth are protected against exploitation and against moral and material abandonment.

The above noted provision of the Indian Constitution provides gender justice, economic justice, social justice, equality or juvenile justice to the society. These six parts of Article 39 speak louder than fundamental rights. Thus, it is quite clear that these provisions, enshrined in Part IV of Indian Constitution, relates to the oppressed, and weaker classes of the society. Article 39A mandates equal justice and free legal aid to the poor by providing that. The state shall secure that the operation of the legal system promotes justice, on a basis of equal opportunity, and shall in particular, provide free legal aid, by suitable legislation or schemes or in any way, to ensure that opportunities for securing justice are not denied to any citizen by reason of economic or other disabilities. This provision of the Constitution is based on the rule of law and Equality before law which is fundamental pillars of democracy, legal aid is considered to be an integral part of administration of justice.

Article 39A speaks apparently legal aid in India has a comprehensive constitutional status and ambit, its inspiration individuality and operation being found in the fascicules of articles its jurisprudential roots socio-legal charter, character and perspective amplitude are evident from the circumstances that we the people of India who are by and large, poor and backward, are at on the architects and beneficiaries of the new order. Legal aid is part of social justice. Social justice demands that when the man lives within the society is he has no source for fighting his case even it is the duty of state to provide the free legal aid.

Article 41 provide for right to work, to education and public assistance in certain Extent. It directs that the state shall, within limit of its economic capacity and development, make effective provision for securing the right to work, to education and to public assistance in cases of unemployment, old age, sickness and disablement, and in other cases of undeserved wants.

Social security is part of social justice. This provision of the Indian Constitution lays stress on social security to aged, orphans and unemployed youths. This provision also speaks about economic rights of an individual. Right to work directly deals with personal liberty or right to life. If you deny this right you deny the person the right to life.

Many studies have shown that with the exception of socialistic countries all other have acute unemployment problems. It is a basic principle of socialism that every one should contribute according to his ability and capability and receive according to his work. But situation is grave in less developed countries. Although directive principles provide for the social and economic security but are economic situation is weak to satisfy these things.

Article 43 speaks about the living way etc. for workers. It provides that the state shall endeavour to secure, by suitable legislation or economic organization or in any other way, to all workers, agricultural, industrial or otherwise, work, a living wage, condition of work ensuring a decent standard of life and full enjoyment of leisure and social cultural opportunities and in particular the state shall endeavour to promote cottage industries on an individual or co-operative basis in rural areas.

This provision of Indian Constitution thus talks about industrial justice or industrial jurisprudence. Various labour law legislation such as, Industrial Dispute Act (1947), Workman Compensation Act (1923), Trade Union Act (1926), Factory Act (1948), Minimum Wages Act (1948), seek to implement this provision of the Constitution.

Article 43A speaks about participation of worker in management of industries. By provisions that the state shall take steps, by suitable legislation or in any other way, to secure the participation of workers in management of undertaking, establishment of other organization engaged in any industry. The insertion of this article opens a new perspective in industrial regulation particularly relating to discharge reinstatement, right to back wages on reinstatement.[52] These provisions also give rights to trade unions to participate with management on the issue of worker's right.

Article 45 provides that state shall endeavour to provide free and compulsory education to children upto the age of fourteen years within a period ten years from the commencement of the Constitution. The provision for free education upto a certain standard or age finds a place in most constitution of the world.[53] Our Constitution-makers are influenced by these provisions and add in the Constitution. Article 21A has given the right to education is a fundamental right.

Organization of Village Self-Government : Article 40

Modernization of agricultural economy prohibition of slaughter of cows and some other cattles: promotion of cottage industry on individual basis and co-operative basis in rural areas. These set of articles present the future framework of rural Indian as comprehend by the founding father. The most of these directive principles reflect the life long teaching of Mahatma Gandhi which was instilled in his follower dominating the constituent assembly is universally

52. D.D. Basu, Shorter Constitution of India, (2003), p. 456.
53. M. Hidaytullah, Constitutional Law of India, (1984), Vol. 1, p. 689.

acknowledged.[54] Because democracy demands the people participation in the process.

Article 46 lays emphasis on the promotion of educational and economic interests of schedule castes schedule tribes and other weaker sections by providing that the state shall promote with special care for the educational and economic interests of the weaker section of the people, and in particular of scheduled castes and schedules tribes and shall protect them from social injustice and all terms of exploitation.

This article embodies the concept of distributive justice which connotes, *inter alia,* removal of an economic inequalities and rectifying the injustice resulting from dealings or transactions between unequal societies.[55] Social justice demands that there should be equality in the society and every body get according to his capacity and need. That is why our Constitution-makers have added these articles in Indian Constitution.

3.3 RELATIONSHIP BETWEEN FUNDAMENTAL RIGHTS AND DIRECTIVE PRINCIPLES

While moving the Constitution first Amendment Bill in 1951 which envisaged the reservation policy, Pandit Nehru observed:

> The Directive Principles of State Policy represent a dynamic move towards a certain objective. The fundamental rights represents something static, to preserve certain rights which exist. Both again are right. But somehow and sometime it may so happen that dynamic movement and the static stand still do not quite fit into each other. There is certain conflict in the two approaches, not inherently, because that was not means, I am quite sure. But there is that slight difficulty and naturally when the courts of land have to consider this matter they have to lay stress more on fundamental rights than on the directive principles. The result is that whole

54. *Ibid.,* p. 696.
55. D.D. Basu, Constitution of India, (2003), p. 458.

purpose behind constitution, which was meant to be a dynamic constitution leading to a certain goal step by step is somewhat hampered and hindered by the static element being emphasized a little more than the dynamic element.[56]

The Fundamental Rights and Directive Principles therefore, are to work in harmony so as to provide as firm base for reconstructing a new society through a peaceful revolution. Both, Fundamental Rights and Directive Principles are instruments of social change. Social revolution is based on these principles. But on the other hand, conflict between fundamental rights and directive principle of state policy has started with commencement of constitution animally because one is based on social good and other is based on the individual good. But Indian Supreme Court has played dynamic role to make reconciliation between these two. Some of these important cases in this regard are discussed hereunder:

> In *State of Madras* v. *S.M. Champkam D. Rajan* AIR 1951 SC 226, Justice Das held that the directive principles of state policy has to conform to run subsidiary to the chapter of fundamental right. In our opinion that is correct way in which the provision found in Parts III and IV have to be understood. Moreover, so long as there is no infringement of any fundamental right, there can be no objection to start acting in accordance with directive principles of state policy set out in Part IV, but subject to again to legislative and executive powers and limitations conferred on the state under the different provision of the Constitution.[57]

The Supreme Court upheld that the validity of 17 Amendments to the Constitution which Gajendragadkar, C.J.,

56. See, M. Hidayatullah, Constitutional Law of India, (1984), Vol. 1, p. 662.
57. AIR 1951 SC 226.

inter alia, observed that parliament is seeking to amendment fundamental rights solely with the object of removing any possible obstacle in the fulfilment of the socio economic policy in which the party in power believes, though no direct reference to any directive principle was made.[58]

In *Golak Nath* v. *State of Punjab*, AIR 1967 SC 1643, Justice hidalyatullah observed that fundamental rights are protected, but directive principles of state policy are not. The former represents the limits of state action and latter are the obligations and duties of the government as a good and socially responsible government. The protection of fundamental right is necessary so that we may not walk in fear of democracy itself. But at the same time it is wrong to invoke the directive principles of state policy as if there is some antimony between them and the fundamental rights.[59]

While the Supreme Court held that the rights conferred under Part III are fundamental, the directive principle given under Part IV are fundamental in the governance of the country. We see no conflict on the whole between the provisions contained in Part III an Part IV. They are complementary and supplementary to each other. The provision of Part IV enables the legislature and the government to impose various duties on citizen. The provisions therein are deliberately made elastic because the duties to be imposed on citizen depend on the extent to which directive principle are implemented. The mandate of Constitution is to build a welfare society in which justice, social, economic and political shall inform all institutions of our national life. The hopes and aspirations aroused by Constitution will be belied if the minimum needs of the lowest of our citizen are not met.[60]

In *Kesavanand Bharti* v. *State of Kerala*, AIR 1973 SC 1461, Justice Mathew observed that the object of the people to establish the Constitution was to promote justice, liberty and equality. The *modus operandi* to achieve these objectives is set out in Parts III and IV of the Constitution. Both Parts III and

58. AIR 1965 SC 845.
59. AIR 1967 SC 643.
60. AIR 1970 SC 2042.

IV enumĕrate certain rights. Each of these parts represents in the main statement in one sense of certain aspirations whose fulfilment was regarded as essential to the kind of society which the Constitution-makers wanted to build. Many articles, whether in Part III or Part IV represents moral rights which they recognized as inherent in every human being. The task of protecting and realizing these rights into socio political realties, some degree of compromise must be present. While referring to observation of Justice Subba Rao in *Golaknath case*, the Supreme Court said that fundamental right, and directive principles of state policy from an integrated whole and were elastic enough to respond to the changing needs of the society.[61]

In *Minerva Mills Ltd.* v. *Union of India*, the Court observed that the Indian Constitution is founded on the bed-rock of the balance between Parts III and IV. To give absolute primacy to one over other is to disturb, the harmony of the Constitution. The harmony and balance between fundamental rights and directive principles is an essential feature of basic structure of the Indian Constitution. Anything that destroys the balance between the two parts will *ipso facto* destroy an essential element of the basic structure of our Constitution.[62]

In *AIR India Statutory Corpn.* v. *United Labour Union*, the Directive Principles of State Policy are fore-runner of the UNO Convention of right to development. These are inalienable human rights, and every person and all people are entitled to participate, contribute to and enjoy economic, social, cultural and political development in which all human rights, fundamental freedoms would be fully realized. Therefore, directive principles how stand elevated to inalienable fundamental human rights. Even they are justifiable by themselves. Social and economic democracy is the foundation for stable political democracy. Therefore, for establishment of just social order in which social economic democracy would be way of life inequalities in income should be removed and every endeavour to be made to eliminate inequalities in status through the rule of law.[63]

61. AIR 1973 SC 1461.
62. AIR 1980 SC 1789.
63. AIR 1997 SC 1277.

The Constitution aim at bringing about a synthesis between fundamental right and directive principle of state policy by giving to a former a place of pride and to the latter a place of performance together they form core of the Constitution. They constitute its true conscience and without faithfully implementing directive principle it is not possible to achieve the welfare contemplated by the Constitution.

In *Unni Krishnan* v. *State of A.P.*, it was observed that this Court has been consistently adopting the approach that the fundamental rights and directive principles are supplementary and complementary to each other and that the provision in Part III should be interpreted having regard to the preamble and directive principle of state policy. The initial hesitation to recognize the profound significance of Part IV has been given up long ago. The Court also referred to the views of Sardar Vallabh Bhai Patel during discussion in the constituent assembly on the interim report on fundamental rights that in Parts III and IV as fundamental rights, one justifiable and the other non-justificiable. In his supplemental report, he stated.[64]

In *Jalu Bhai Nana Bhai Kachar* v. *State of Gujarat,* the Court held that it is accordingly clear that in a welfare state envisioned in the directive principle of state policy the basic equalities are the every one entitled to minimum material well-being, such as food, clothing and decent housing. A living standard is possible with existing or expanding physical resources and scientific knowledge, etc. and state has right and duty to act when private initiative fails.

In a democratic society, every individual need, legal protection for beneficial enjoyment of what he has discovered and appropriated; has created by his own labour and what he has acquired under existing socio-economic conditions subject to law and order. Equality welfare consist in adjusting individual interest with social interest by aid of law as social engineering which would mean public restraint on property designed to mitigate the privilege which property offer enjoyment of the things that life has offer. Restraint on power of command as a means of quasi government private control over is major asset of nation. The directive principles enjoins

64. AIR 1993 SC 2178.

the state to re-organize the economic system by the law or administrative means and fundamental rights are means to that end to give right to life to be meaningful, equality of opportunity and status of dignity of a person of reality. The fundamental right and directive principle are two wheels of the chariot as aid to make social and economic democracy a truism.[65]

In *Markendya* v. *State of A.P.*, AIR 1989 SC 1308, the Court observed that Article 39(b), contained in Part IV of the Constitution, ordains the state to direct its policy towards securing equal pay for equal work for both men and women. Provision contained in chapter on the directive principles of state policy cannot be enforced by Constitution although the principle contained there are fundamental in nature for governance of our country. The court has no power to direct the legislature to frame laws to give effect to directive principles as contained in Part IV of the Constitution or to in just the legislature from making such law. But while considering question of enforcement of fundamental right of citizen it is open to the court to be guided by directive principles contained 'these in are maintained. The purpose of Article 39(d) is to fix certain social and economic goals for avoiding only discrimination amongst the citizen doing similar work in matter relating to pay, the court must strike down discrimination and direct to state to adhere to the doctrine of equal pay and equal work as enshrined under Article 39(d) of the Constitution.[66]

The Supreme Court has thus played a dynamic role in interpreting fundamental rights and directive principles of the state policy. Supreme Court in its various judgments has made it clear that these are two pillars which are complementary and supplementary to each other. Social justice is possible in the society only when these pillars work together. It is clear that the directive principles form the fundamental features and the social conscience of the Constitution and the Constitution enjoins upon the State to implement these directive principles. So far as Court's are concerned where there is no apparent

65. AIR 1995 SC 142, para 47.
66. AIR 1989 SC 1308.

inconsistency between the directive principles contained in Part IV and fundamental rights mentioned in Part III which supplement each other, there is no difficulty inputting harmonious constitution which advance the object of the Constitution.[67]

3.4 JUSTICE V.R. KRISHNA IYER'S VIEWS ON RELATIONSHIP BETWEEN FUNDAMENTAL RIGHTS AND DIRECTIVE PRINCIPLES AND CONCEPT OF SOCIAL JUSTICE

According to Justice Chinappa Reddy Krishna Iyer is keenly alive to great importance of the directive principles and that he has accepted them as code of interpretation to construe the Constitution and the laws. And fundamentals rights have never meant to constitutional barrier of social reform.[68]

Parts III and IV of the Constitution provide a panorama of legislative concern. That is why Krishna Iyer says that directive principles of State Policy which mandate the administration to promote the welfare of the people by securing a progressive social order are no longer a pious wish package but a programme of action. Krishna Iyer holds that larger purpose of our constitutional directive in Parts III and IV is the higher values which are finer strands of our composite cultural heritage and the fulfilment by determined legal direction of the evolution of rising expectation of the masses—these alone make jurisprudence sociologically valid and legislation communally legitimate.[69]

Naturally the cardinal question arises what are the vital values of constitutional transformation. Parts III and IV are the warp and root of the fabric of our national charter and project the radical ideology of a system of activist equals, human dignity and fundamental freedom in setting of a dynamic participative democracy with an egalitarian social milieu in

67. Sherful Hussain, Supreme Court on Fundamental Rights and Directive Principles, (1981), p. 68.
68. See, Shilja Chander, Justice V.R. Krishna Iyer on Directive Principle and Fundamental Rights, (1998), p. 72.
69. *Ibid.*, p. 73.

which the full and free development of every individual is basic. Broad socio-economic humanism eradicating poverty, an arithmatizing concentration of wealth and natural resources ensuring fair living condition for every one and sentencing to death anti social, exploitative and authoritarian manipulation of state and society. These are our Fabian get militant ambition.[70]

Iyer is of the opinion that the question then is about the quintessence and quantum of the constitutional mandate luminously abbreviated in the preamble but radically broadened in Parts III and IV. We must understand that founding fathers were persons with vision and pathetic passion.[71]

In the views of Krishna Iyer directive principles are based on social good but fundamental rights are based on individual good that is why Iyer says that fundamental right deals with capitalistic society and directive principles deals with weaker section of the society. Iyer lays stress on directive principles and for their implementation. In the case of:

> Justice Iyer Reiterated his views again in *Bhim Singh* v. *UOI*, AIR 1981 SC 234 where he held that Part IV which seek to build a social justice society is basic to our constitutional order. According to him any transgression of Article 39(b)(c) by any statute would not be valid. Similar views were expressed by justice Iyer in Waman Rao, AIR 1981 SC 271, Justice Iyer constituted the bench with Chandrechud (CJ), P.N. Bhagwati, V.D. Tulzpurkar and A.P. Sen J.J. and held that Article 39(b) and (c) contain directive principle which are vital to the well-being of the country and welfare of its people. So it is impossible to conceive that any law passed for such a purpose can at all violate Articles 14 and 19.[72]

70. V.R. Krishna Iyer, Justice and Beyond Law (1982), p. 33.
71. V.R. Krishna Iyer, A Random Miscellany Legal and Others, (1984), p. 62.
72. See Shilja Chander, Justice B.R. Krishna Iyer on Directive Principles and Fundamental Rights, (1998), p. 77.

In *M.H. Quarshi* v. *State of Bihar*, justice Iyer held that a harmonious interpretation has to be placed upon the Constitution and so interpreted it means that the state should certainly implement the directive principle but it must do so in such a way that its law do not take away or abridge the fundamental rights for otherwise the protecting provision of chapter III will be mere robe in sand.[73]

Iyer holds the view that directive principles are based on the concept of social justice. Iyer says that when we talk about social justice we have to implement these principles. According to justice Iyer today world has become so complex and every where we see competition and man has become instrument to get materialistic things. State has entered into the era of *laissez faire* which supports the capitalistic society; labour has become instrument of exploitation and due to this rich has become richer and poor become poorer. In business or contact under the existing system one cannot expected social justice realizing social justice government has to implement both elements and only then social justice is possible.

Krishna Iyer says that in order to realize social justice we have to make harmonious construction between two pillars of the Constitution. Any government cannot ignore them. Man's existence depends upon social existence and if we get socio-economic right then there is no need for other rights. If we get success in the implementation of these principles then fundamental rights get implemented automatically. But for this we have to start the movement for the implementation of these directive principles only then social justice is possible in the society. On October 31, 2007 justice V.R. Krishna Iyer wrote a letter to West Bengal Governor on Nandigram issue and wrote that: we are no longer feudal or colonial and must generate a great fulfilment of social justice and distributive development which is first promise of our Constitution and paramount obligation of Swaraj.

Iyer wrote that West toxicated industrial renaissance is the only salvation from privation for Indian humanity. A magnificent compromise between these two rival views is possible if state violence for land acquisition and terrorism of

---

73. *Ibid.*, p. 77.

untruly hostile political element taking law into their hands and controlled with social justice goal. That is statesmanship through creative policy revolution. Iyer further said that development is not thing but man. This is how justice Iyer talks about balance between social good and individual good. Therefore, he always lays stress on the implementation of directive principles.[74]

3.5 SUM UP

Directive Principles of State Policy and fundamental rights are the two pillars of Indian democracy. Without one other is not possible; both are complementary and supplementary to each other. Indian Supreme Court has played the dynamic role in the conciliation of the provisions of fundamental rights and directive principles. Social justice is only possible when we are able to implement these both. Parts III and IV together reflect the philosophy of our constitution. These principles reveal that our Constitution-makers wanted to set socialistic pattern. However, one thing is quite obvious that the Constitution of India is neither democratic on western line nor socialistic on the line formed by communist countries. No doubt, the makers of the Constitution of India were influenced by the principle of Marxism, but they were not ready to sacrifice democratic elements just for sake of Marxism.[75] That is why they adopted democratic socialism.

In democratic socialism it is essential to maintain a balance between social good and individual good. That is why both directive principles and fundamental rights are enshrined in the Constitution. Iyer's concept relating to relationship between fundamental rights and directive principles is very clear. He holds the opinion that they are complementary and supplementary to each other. For social justice there is a need to make balance between these two. Iyer says that we should interpret the Constitution by keeping in view socio-economic conditions of the society.

74. V.R. Krishna Iyer, An Open Letter to West Bengal Governor on October 31, 2007, *The Hindu*, Saturday, November 3, 2007.
75. Chandrika Singh, Constitutional Battle in India, (2001), p. 35.

4

Judicial Postulates and Krishna Iyer's Concept of Social Justice

Foremost among humanitarian qualities of Krishna Iyer was his love for his fellowmen. He gave new orientation to the justicing process and innovated what we may call poverty jurisprudence or Dalit jurisprudence. He regarded the law as an instrument of social engineering, a powerful tool in the hands of society for the purpose of reaching social justice to the common man. He always held the little Indian in his mind and whatever he did or said judicially was directly solely towards improving the life condition of the large masses of people in the country suffering from want and destitution.[1]

There is no wrong if we say that Justice V.R. Krishna Iyer the Everest of the Indian Bench during his era. He always believed that law cannot afford to remain a brooding omnipotence in the sky but it must become the law in action. He often said that law is what law does.[2]

1. P. Krishnaswamy, Justice V.R. Krishna Iyer, A Living Legend, 2004, p. 373.
2. M.P.R. Nair, Justice Krishna Iyer at 90, 2005, p. 27.

For him life is a sacred trust with a deep obligation to do one's best in this world. For him life is a verb not noun. The journey of life is not a mechanical flow of time. It is dynamic march towards nobler incarnation, transforming the current chaos into a sublime cosmos.[3]

Few men have participated as fully in the public life of their time as Justice V.R. Krishna Iyer possessed of one of the great provincial fortunes, he is a handsome and graceful man, regarding by his contemporaries as modest and cultivated. He has an extra-ordinary record of public service. In his political and judicial career one major assignment followed another with kaleidoscopic variety and swiftness. He is lover of books and his ideas had formed a reality and allure the most associate with material things. Above all he was endowed with the priceless but often dangerous quality, creative imagination. His mind reached out and grasped concept beyond the horizons of orthodox belief.

As William Blake so poignantly portrays in his poem 'Agonies of Innocence'

> Every night and every morn
> Some mystery are born
> Every morn and every night
> Some are born to sweep delight
> Some are born to endless night[4]

Justice V.R. Krishna Iyer is close friend of Dalits. In his one judgment he gave birth to a new concept which is known as Dalit jurisprudence. Justice Krishna Iyer has given some modest dynamic judgments in legal history of the Supreme Court of India. For him courts are kidney of the whole legal system. Therefore, he never misses the opportunity to deliver the judgment in favour of common man. During the tenure, most of his judgments are based on social justice.

The justice system across the motion must be made accessible to the poor and the handicapped that are currently priced out the court and tribunals. When people talk about

3. Justice V.R. Krishna Iyer, Judge Postpouri, 2007, p. 93.
4. Justice V.R. Krishna Iyer, Legally Speaking (2004), p. 120.

access to justice, they may mean many different things depending on their ethos and socio-economic history and developmental potential. The tryst with destiny made when India won independence emphasized the alleviation of poverty and inequality which are aspects of economic injustice. Therefore, our jurisprudence must possess a vision of this social philosophy.[5]

Justice in the Indian context must be a people-oriented. The people are poor, socially suppressed, illiterate and steeped in rural backwardness. Any judicial reform package must cognize the people factor, their village base, the feudal pyramid and urban extortion. The Constitution has injected the spirit of right, evolution and equal justice. So class justice is a cost cause and long-run and upper berth. Justicing art must be given a long holiday. Human rights postulate the right to life, to human dignity to creatures comforts to cultural personhood for everyone.[6]

Justice V.R. Krishna Iyer was also in favour of industrial justice and industrial jurisprudence. Many of his judgments are regarded with industrial matters. He wanted to finish the eternal conflict between capital and labour. He wanted to abolish the death punishment. His pro-humanism approach made him famous in legal history of India. He always pleaded that courts are laboratory where the law has been tested. Law is a human institution.

Humanism is the justification for many ameliorative methodologies favouring the have-nots and marginalized. For every human voice had democratic rights it is fundamental that provisions are made to convert every person into governor of the country.[7]

Moreover, human beings have always wondered what the future has store in them. They have also wondered whether it can be divided in all. When mankind was in its infancy,

---

5. The Dynamics of Access to Justice by V.R. Krishna Iyer, *The Hindu*, Tuesday, May 29, 2007.
6. V.R. Krishna Iyer, A Random Miscellany Legal and Other, 1998, p. 15.
7. Justice V.R. Krishna Iyer, Democracy and Election Process, *The Hindu*, Wednesday, 4th July, 2007.

attempt to predict the future was made from the position of the stars and planets, and by means of other similarity naïve method, which of course, could not be too reliable. Justice V.R. Krishna Iyer says that economic is base of social life. Law has grown out of economic structure.

4.1 JUSTICE IYER AND HIS JUDICIAL VIEW REGARDING SOCIAL JUSTICE

According to Justice V.R. Krishna Iyer, Indian Constitution is a human document; main base of the Constitution is administration of justice. During freedom struggle of India ten of thousands people have been killed indifferent phases and one million people exchanged when the partition has taken place between India and Pakistan. The Constitution of India is laden with social justice not to be whittled down by semantic scaling down or pedantic play of interpretation. On the contrary, it is value loaded with social concern and provides for discrimination in favour of socially and educationally backward class as well as Scheduled Castes and Tribes. Democracy with equality, on a level playing ground is never achieved where oasis of elite upper class are able to prosper leaving sandy deserts of destitute of under privileged in a state of despair.[8]

Constitution of India promises social economic equality or political equality. Constitution is not document of 98,000 words but it is conscience of Indian people. Indian Constitution starts with five dynamic words 'We the People of India' which reveals the concept of popular sovereignty. When we study judgments of justice Krishna Iyer his concept of social justice is very deeply concerned with people and common man. In *E. Annamma* v. *State of A.P.*,[9] Justice Iyer says that:

> The humanism of our Constitution, echoing the concern of the universal declaration of human rights is deeply concerned about the worth of human person. Justice Iyer dictates that "We assume that a better world is one

8. Justice V.R. Krishna Iyer, Human Rights—A Judge's Miscellany, (1995), p. 42.
9. AIR 1974 SC 799.

without legal knifing of life, given proposition of social change. Even so to sublimate savagery in individual or society is a long experiment in spiritual chemistry where moral value, social and economic conditions and legislative judgment have role.[10] This case dealt with death penalty.

4.2 JUSTICE IYER'S VIEWS ON LAW AND JUSTICE

Iyer law is seldom talking term of justice. The purpose of law is success of justice. Main subject of law is to provide justice. Law is a human institution mad by human agents, satisfying human wants. But Justice Iyer says that in Indian context law is technical word which differ from society. But law and society both are co-related to each other. Law is not above the society. It grows within the society and goes away as society go. Justice Iyer says that law is satellite of economic structure.

The Constitution of India is a social, human or kind document of social justice. It is based on concept of welfare state and social good. Law in print is not justice in life until each man realizes what justice due to him is. Therefore, he always dictates same line of Justice Coke, 'be ever you high but law is above you'. He always dictates these lines in his book "Law, Society and Collective Consciousness."

"Law without justice is blind
Justice without law is lame;
Law geared to justice is order."

Mission of law is to provide justice. Iyer's concept relating to law is very dynamic. Law is based on social-economic conditions. It means that if production and distribution is in hands of general public than law has relevancy. Rule of law should be close to rule of life. Law and life both are co-related to each other; both are complementary and supplementary to each other. But today if we apply test of

10. *Id.*

V.R. Krishna Iyer then we will find that social justice has become costlier item. Today we follow the foreign and comparative jurisprudence in interpreting our domestic law, but tour social-economic condition is different from each other. There is latent violation of law particularly in the field of labour jurisprudence. If we see the world jurisprudence then we will find that after 1920 whole jurisprudence of world has changed. Today all the countries of the world pursue the pure theory of law. Because after the 1920 we are going towards contract or business-oriented society, where the social justice is only myth or unforeseen reality. After 1920 we are enter into consumerist or materialistic society, where the economics is everything. But Constitution of India is based on sociological school. But in today's era social justice became paper tiger. Law has become one sided and has single mind approach towards human beings.

Justice Iyer has criticized the law in present system which is against the human beings. Therefore, during his era of judgeship he was always in favour of industrial jurisprudence. Therefore, Iyer quoted the lines of Antotle France in his many books. "To disarm the strong and arm the weak would be to change the social order which it is my job to preserve. Justice is the mean by which established injustices are sanctioned."[11]

It is fundamental to our constitutional scheme that justice social, economic and political is the final aim of the government. Individual justice is integral, not expendable and so no one shall be unjustly treated in his several, spiritual, social economic and political relation.[12] But according to Justice Iyer legal justice has become teasing illusion between reality and promise. Justice has become market commodity. Law has become instrument in the hands of few people. Law is an instrument, not an end. Justice is its function and its validation. If there is nothing to hope from the law there may be short against the law, and if injustice is legalized, insurrection will rise. Law is under justice not above.[13] Iyer while referring Marxian Jurisprudence quoted:

11. V.R. Krishna Iyer, Equal Justice and Forensic Process Truth and Myth, (1986), p. 4.
12. V.R. Krishna Iyer, Law Versus Justice, (1981), p. 15.
13. *Ibid.*, p. 23.

> Your jurisprudence is but the will of your class made into a law for all, a will, whose essential character and direction are determined by economic condition of existence of your class.

The judicial process of Indian legal system is very old which has symptoms of colonial government. We have penal justice system of 150 years old and there is wide gap between law and society, but we are unable to change that antique law. Iyer is of the opinion that there is need for revision of whole legal system, but before this there is need to change the social-economic condition of the society. Our Constitution is based on democratic process, in that situation we need democratic legal system. But our legal system is such that people are always afraid to go in the Court because of time consuming process and giving mental stress to a person who becomes victim of court. Such type of mechanism is harmful for the society and concept of social justice which is given by the Constitution of India, i.e. "no cause is more worthy than cause of human rights or more than legal concepts; they are essence of man. They are what make man human. That is why they are called human rights, deny them you deny man's humanity."[14]

Law should be honest, simple and people oriented. The purpose of law should be to give justice to the people. "The purpose of law and purpose of judiciary is not merely to sit in wig and gown for a number of hours a day and look very learned. They supply a social purpose that is, to bring about justice, to deliver justice to the people."[15]

Purpose of law is to provide public benefit rather than punishment but in Indian system law is just like terror to the people. People follow the law because of punishment rather than for social benefit. Law must be like a medicine, as and when we are in fever, get the medicine and get relief from fever. But in Indian system law is like ivory tower which has no relation with justice system. Our legal system provides justice according to law, not law according to justice. Therefore, T.S. Eilot says:

---

14. V.R. Krishna Iyer, Legally Speaking, (Rer. 2004), p. 130.
15. *Ibid.*, p. 146.

"Where there is life, we lost in living?
Where there is wisdom, we lost in knowledge?
Where there is knowledge, we have lost in information.

Same story has happened with Indian legal system. Indian legal Darwinism has one sided approach and social justice became mockery for our constitutional order and legal system. To wipe tears from every eye the noble Gandhian though has become a thought for coming generation. Therefore, this line of King Martin Luther is very suitable in that situation, "we guided the missiles, but misguide the man".

The concept of man is very difficult to understand. Law is not above human values, human sentiments and emotions of a person. Law can never be higher than economic order and cultural development of society brought to pass by that economic order. Functioning of law is to balance of interest in the society. The rule of law, view in its progressive perspective, has thus a ridicule mission.

> "The rule of law is a dynamic concept for expansion and fulfilment. Jurists are primarily responsible and which should be employed not only to safeguard and advance the civil and political rights of individual in free society, but also establish social, economic, educational and cultural condition under which legitimate aspirations and dignity may be realized."[16]

Dr. Ambedkar in Constituent Assembly said that:

> Indeed if I may say so, if things under new Constitution the reason will not be that we had bad Constitution, what we will have to say is that man was vile.[17]

Justice Krishna Iyer also gives stress on human nature. For him life is not verb but noun, it is perennial process but not a final product. Law is organic science if it satisfies maximum needs of human beings in the society. Role of

16. V.R. Krishna Iyer, Legally Speaking, (2004), p. 149.
17. *Ibid.*

judiciary must be third eye in democratic process. John Ruskin said that, "I hold it for indisputable, that the first duty of the state is to see that every child born therein shall be well housed, fed, education till it attain years of discretion".

This is function of law. Judges are oracle of society. They guide the society and estimated forthcoming problem before the nation judiciary should be fiduciary towards the people. It is function of the judge to draw out the actual meaning of the law. Statutes are Skelton but this is filled up by interpreting the law. There is nothing wrong, if we say that courts are laboratories where the law has been tested. Judges must adopt he pro-humanism approach towards society's common man.

4.3 IYER'S VIEW ON PRISON JUSTICE

Justice V.R. Krishna Iyer also co-regulates the prison justice system to social justice and constitutional values which are enshrined in our Raj Dharma.

Convicts are not mere reason of the conviction denuded of all fundamental rights which they otherwise possess. A compulsion under the authority of law following upon a conviction to live in a prison house entails by its own force the deprivation of fundamental freedom like the right to move truly throughout the territory of India or right to practice a profession. But the Constitution guarantees other freedoms like right to acquire hold and dispose of property for exercise of which incarceration can be no impediment. Likewise, even a convict is entitled to the precious right guaranteed by Article 21 of the Constitution that he shall not be deprived of his life and personal liberty except according to procedure established by law.[18] There are some landmark judgments regarding prison justice system by Justice Krishna Iyer.

In *Sunil Batra* v. *Delhi Administration*,[19] Justice Iyer observed that, prisoners are still 'persons' entitled to all constitutional rights unless their liberty has been constitutionally curtailed by procedures that satisfy all the requirements of due process. There is no irony curtain drawn

18. V.R. Krishna Iyer, Human Rights—A Judge Miscellany, (1975), p. 94.
19. AIR 1978 SC 1675.

between the Constitution and prison of this country. Conviction of a crime does not render one a non person whose rights are subject to the whim of the prison administration, and therefore, the imposition of any serious punishment within the prison system requires procedural safeguards.

Social justice in the prison context has a functional versality hardly explored. The roots of our Constitution lie deep in the finer spiritual source of social justice, beyond the melting pot of bad politicking feudal crudities and sublimated sadism sustaining itself by profound faith in man and his latent divinity and the confidence that you can accomplish by kindness what you cannot do by force.

Rule of law is important in the stability of society. Arbitrary action in revocation of paroles can only impede and impair the rehabilitative aspects of modern penology. Notice and opportunity for hearing appropriate to the nature of the case are the rudiments of due process which restore the faith that our society is run for the many, not for few, and that fair dealing rather than caprice will govern the affairs of man.

If our laws were to reflect a higher respect for life, restraint of the person is justified only if the potential harm is considerable.[20] The law is not abracadabra but at once pragmatic and astute and does not surrender its power before scary exaggerations of security by prison bosses.[21]

Social justice cannot sleep if the Constitution hangs limp where its consumers most need its humanism. Social justice requires that before a law can become operative it must be promulgated or published. It must be broadcast in some recognizable way so that all men know what it is.

Freedom behind bars' is part of our constitutional tryst and the index of our collective consciousness. That the flower of human divinity never fades is part of our cultural heritage.

In *Moti Ram* v. *State of M.P.*,[22] Justice Krishna Iyer observes that the law in its majestic equality forbids the rich as well as poor to sleep under bridges, to beg in the street and to steel bread. Social Justice is the signature tune of our

20. *Id.*
21. *Id.*
22. AIR 1978 SC 1595.

Constitution and the little man in peril of losing his liberty is the consumer of Social Justice.

The above noted case deals with bail and bond. In this case a person was unable to deposit surety of bail therefore, he was in jail. In this judgment Justice Krishna Iyer criticized the Indian criminal justice system and the person was released on bail.

In *Jolly George Varghese and Another* v. *Bank of Cochin*,[23] Justice V.R. Krishna Iyer said that to be poor in this land of Dridra Narayan (land of poverty) is no crime and to recover debt by procedure of putting one in prison is flagrantly violative of Article 21 of the Constitution unless there is proof of minimal fairness of his wilful failure to pay in spite of his insufficient means and absence of more terribly pressing claim on his means such as medical bill to treat concern or other grave illness.

In *Prem Shankar Shukla* v. *Delhi Administration*,[24] dealing with the handcuffing Justice V.R. Krishna Iyer laid down that, access to human justice is the essence of Article 32, and sensitized by this dynamic perspective we have examined the facts and the law and the rival versions of the petitioner and the Delhi Administration. The blurred area of 'detention jurisprudence' where considerations of prevention of escape and personhood of prisoner come into conflict, warrants fuller exploration than this isolated case necessitates and counsel on both sides.

He further held that handcuffing is *prima facie* inhuman and, therefore, unreasonable, is over-harsh and at the first flush, arbitrary. Absent fair procedure and objective monitoring, to inflict 'irons' is to resort to zoological strategies repugnant to Article 21.

4.4 JUSTICE V.R. KRISHNA IYER AND RESERVATION POLICY

Justice Iyer has also give a remarkable judgment on distributive justice. Therefore, in one of the case he discussed the nature of law.

23. AIR 1980 SC 470.
24. AIR SC 1535.

In *N.K. Chauhan* v. *State of Gujarat*,[25] Justice Krishna Iyer observed that the law must be precise, simple, clear, comprehensive and this is duty on the law maker at every level not to injure the community by longed webs of rules, order and notification whose meaning revealed only through transcendental meditation or constant litigation. In socialistic pattern of society there is hardly any part of rational life or personal life which is not attracted by some legal rules or other. When man have to look the law form candle to grave making subsidiary laws demands greatest attention.

In *State of Kerala* v. *N.M. Thomas*,[26] Justice V.R. Krishna Iyer states that law including constitutional law, can no longer do it alone but must be illumined in the interpretative process by sociology and allied field of knowledge. Indeed the term constitutional law symbolizes an intersection of law and politics where an issue of political power are acted on by person trained in legal tradition working in judicial institution.

Moreover, Constitution of India is a great social document, almost revolutionary in its aim of transforming a medieval, hierarchical society into a modern, equalitarian democracy.

Social engineering which is law in action—must adopt new strategies to liquidate entrusted group injustice of surrender society to traumatic tension. My touchstone is that functional democracy prostitutes participation by all section of people and their representation in administration in an index of such participation.

He further observed that the Preamble to the Constitution silhouettes a 'justice-oriented' community. The Directive Principles of State Policy, fundamental in the governance of the country, enjoin on the State the promotion "with special care the educational and economic interests of the weaker sections of the people, and, in particular, of the Scheduled Castes and the Scheduled Tribes, and protect them from social injustice. Equal opportunity is a hope, not a menace.

In *A.B.S.K. Sangh Rly.* v. *Union of India*,[27] Justice Krishna Iyer quoted Leo N. Tolostey who said that, "the abolition of

25. AIR 1977 SC 257.
26. AIR SC 490.
27. AIR 1981 SC 298.

slavery has gone on far long time Rome abolished slavery, America abolished it, and we did but only the words were abolished not the things."

Justice Iyer observed that the dynamic and diabetics of social justice *vis-a-vis* the special provision of Constitution calculated to accelerate the prospects of employment of harijans and girjans in civil service with particular emphasis on promotion of these categories in India Railway.

We must make our political democracy as social democracy as well. Political democracy cannot last unless these lies at base of it social democracy.

To make democracy functional and the republic real the social and economic personality of these backward most sections had to be restored. From this angle, the ancient injustice on the shudras among the shudras has to be liquidated by effective equalizing measures. Power, material power, is the key to socio-economic salvation and the State being the nidus of power, the framers of the Constitution have made provision for representation of these weaker sections both in the legislature and the executive.

> "Great things are done when men and mountains meet; this is not done by jostling in the street."

4.5 IYER'S VIEWS ON CRIMINAL JUSTICE

There is a stage for formulation of first principle in the field of crime and punishment at once spiritually informed medically instructed, divinely valuated and judicially mandated and beyond all these, impressed with the fine humanism of international instrument and luminous jurisprudence of human right. It is believed that:

Criminals are made, not born, are curably human not irredeemably brutish. Justice Krishna Iyer treated prisoners as patients. He believed in reformative theory of punishment. He correlated rule of law with rule of life. Therefore, in one of his judgment in *State of Punjab* v. *Amar Singh*,[28] he discussed the nature of law in this way:

28. AIR 1974 SC 994.

> "We have to bear in mind the activist though inarticulate major promise in statutory Constitution, the rule of law must run close to the rule of life and court must read into an enactment language permitting that meaning which promote that benignant intent of legislation to one which perverts the scheme of statute on imputed legislative presumption and assume social value valid in prior era."[29]

The main subject of punishment is reform the person, not take revenge which he committed the crime. Therefore, Justice V.R. Krishna Iyer started reformative theory of punishment. In some judgments he took liberal view in giving punishment. He advocated constitutional rights for prisoners. Legal Darwinism is necessary for social development.

In *Charles Sobraj* v. *Superintendent Central Jail, Tihar,*[30] Justice Krishna Iyer said that imprisonment was not spell farewell to fundamental right although by a Republic re-appraisal court will refuse to recognize the full panoply of Part III enjoined by citizens. Fair procedure is the soul of Article 21. Law is essentially the formal expression of regulation.

Man's existence depends upon social structure. Man is made by the society. Therefore, man is not born criminal but made by society. Therefore, prison justice system demands that these procedural and constitutional safeguards shall be adopted by authority. Main function of law is to provide the social development by protecting individual interest. Law is practical mechanism not philosophical method to handle the grave situation. Social justice demands that there must be constitutional safeguard for prisoners. They are also human and have emotional and sentimental values.

Iyer is also against death punishment. In *Bachan Singh* v. *State of Punjab,*[31] court observed that death punishment should be awarded only in rarest of rare case. The rarest of rare case doctrine leaving much too judicial discretion has caused by inner conflict in the mind of judges.

---

29. *Id.*
30. AIR 1978 SC 1514.
31. AIR 1980 SC 898.

But Justice Iyer gave punishment in white collar crime or economic offences. Because he believed that by this offence you snatch the justice from innocent man. In *M.H. Hoskot* v. *State of Maharashtra*,[32] he observed that soft sentencing justice is gross injustice where many innocent are potential victims. He gave grave punishment in such type of offences.

Iyer has pro-humanism approach towards down-trodden people. He has given liberal interpretation regarding the right of such segment of the society. Therefore, in one of judgment in *P.N. Kaushal* v. *Union of India*,[33] referring William Howard Taft he quoted:

> If the law is but essence of common sense the protests of many average men rely evidence a defeat in legal conclusion though based on the nicest legal reasoning and profoundest learning.

If we draw the conclusion about the Iyer concept of social justice and law then we can say that "Law is a human institution made by human agent satisfying human wants" or in other words it can be said that nothing is above human beings. Law is servant of man not master of man. It becomes master only when man goes beyond the power of social system. Social justice can be concluded that when the man lives within society he must be treated fairly and equally and there should be no discrimination on the basis of anything.

Therefore in one of his judgment in *Bar Council* v. *M.V. Dubholkar*,[34] while discussing nature of law Justice Krishna Iyer observed that, law is not trade brief no merchandise and so the heaven of commercial competition or procurement should not vulgarize the legal profession.

Justice cannot be attained without the stream being pellucid through its course and that is of great public concern not mere professional cure.

The conscience of law is administration of justice according to society. Today we have same Constitution like

32. AIR 1978 SC 1548.
33. AIR 1976 SC 1457.
34. AIR 1976 SC 242.

American but interpretation is different due to socio-economic conditions.

Justice V.R. Krishna Iyer was against the death penalty. He wanted to abolish death punishment. He believed in reformative theory of punishment. In many cases he gave dissenting opinion regarding death punishment.

In *Mohammed Giasudin* v. *State of A.P.*,[35] Justice Krishna Iyer was of the view that progressive criminologist across the world will agree that the Gandhian diagnosis of offender as patient and his conception of prison as hospital mental and moral—is the key to the pathology of delinquency and the therapeutic role of punishment. The whole man is healthy man and every man is born well. Criminality is a curable deviance; our prison should be correctional house, not cruel iron aching soul.

If you treat a man like an animal, then you must expect him to act like one. For every action, there is reaction. This is only human nature and in order or an inmate to act like a human being you must trust him as such.

Law is not formal herbal not logomachy but a working technique of justice.

In *Shiv Mohan Singh* v. *State of Delhi*,[36] Justice Krishna Iyer said that the literature on doing justice at the sentencing stage is profound and proliferating and penological controversy on death penalty had led to great dive among sociologist, jurist and spiritualists.

Death is not only an unusually sever punishment, unusual in its pain in its finality and in its enormity, but it serves no purpose more effectively than a less severe punishment, therefore, the principle inherent in the clause that prohibit profitless inflicting of excessive punishment can adequately achieve the same purpose invalidates the punishment.

He further quoted that a learned writer in Indian Constitution has observed:

> Judges must enforce the laws, whatever they be, and decide according to the best of their rights, but the laws

35. AIR 1977 SC 1926.
36. AIR 1977 SC 949.

are not always just and hights are not always luminous, nor again are judicial method always adequate to secure justice.

In the cases *Rajindra Singh* v. *State of U.P.*,[37] *Kanju Kanju Janarthana* v. *State of Kerala*,[38] *Shiv Shankar Dubey* v. *Vitor*,[39] and the Bench while delivering the judgment described in an elaborate manner under what circumstances and for what reasons this cruel death sentence could be imposed.

Law must be honest to itself. It is true that some Judges count number of total wounds, some the nature of weapons used, other count the corpus or the degree of horror and yet other took into age or sex of the offender and even the lapse of time between trial court's award the death punishment and final disposal of case. Gandhiji said, "Only God has right to take away a life because He is God who gave life."

4.6 IYER'S VIEWS ON GENDER JUSTICE

Human history is history of struggle and political and social emancipation. Iyer is also in favour of gender justice. Iyer's concept of gender justice demand full participation of women in political, social and economic field. If we evaluate the historical dialectism than we find that in big epoch of Hindu Mythology supported women's right. In Mahabharata we seek Kunti Putra Ganga Putra it means that women were strong at that time. In present scenario we worship Lakshmi and Sarswati. But in practical situation of gender justice is deteriorating day by day. Iyer always supported gender justice. Our is sacred soil where women are venerated as Sakti and Goddess. There are more deities in our pantheon than male divinities. Nevertheless, we squeeze the life our infant girl immediately after birth.[40]

37. See, P. Krishna Swamy, Justice V.R. Krishna Iyer : A Living Legend, (2004).
38. *Ibid.*
39. *Ibid.*
40. P. Krishnaswamy, Justice V.R. Krishna Iyer a Livng Legend, (Repr. 2004), p. 226.

Socially weaker and economically poorer women of ancient home of many religions, culture and civilization are harshest hit with their human person, treated like commodities, exported, forced to play comfort women, enslaved in brothel and cruelty and carnally subject to sex severities while liberation and actualization of women's equal status and human rights are but tantalizing legal paper.[41]

The most distressing and malignant violation derogatory to dignity of women is related to forced marriage, fraudulent trafficking, coerced prostitutions and denial of the basic purity and moral sanctity of personhood sans which womanhood becomes nothing but lascivious flesh alive only for depraved military eroticism.[42]

Justice Krishna Iyer says that social justice demand gender justice. There should be equal participation of women in every field. Gender justice has a high place in Indian criminal jurisprudence. Civilized jurisprudence entails equal rights and duties towards citizen irrespective of any discrimination. On the other hand, Constitution of India talks about uniform civil code applicable to the whole humanity but after 60 years of independence this work remains unfinished. Justice Krishna Iyer has supported right of Muslim women and demanded uniform civil code for all sections of people in the country. When we talk about "We the People of India" then why we are afraid of uniform civil code. In civil jurisprudence, criminal jurisprudence even than prison jurisprudence also talks about the gender justice. Under Constitution of India equality is basic of constitutional jurisprudence.

One question is also raised that Indian economy is agriculture economy where the rights of women are small in nature. But as industrial section gong on and women becoming aware about their rights, but effect of industrialization is one sided. Therefore, Justice V.R. Krishna Iyer says that "development does not mean that goods which are provided by you, but are calculated by education, discipline or organization."

41. V.R. Krishna Iyer, Human Right—A Judge Miscellany, (1995), p. 150.
42. V.R. Krishna Iyer, Human Right Judge's Miscellany, (1995), p. 152.

The Indian freedom struggle is an unfinished mission until our mothers, sisters and daughters are restored to their social, economic, political and cultural dignity in reality. The rule of law is at service of rule of life and battle for justice for women must begin with gender jurisprudence which salvage the weaker sex equalize her status and organizes her role in society in such a manner that fair partnership in all walks of life.[43]

Constitutional jurisprudence wants to abolish discrimination between men and women. The struggle for Indian jurisprudence was also struggle for women emancipation. Justice through his judgments whether in *Somnath case*[44] or *Narthom Singh* v. *State of Punjab*,[45] or whether *Shahulhumendu* v. *Sahan, Hem Dev* v. *Shubha Beevi*,[46] Justice Krishna Iyer has adopted the dynamic law for gender jurisprudence and justice. He also wrote open letter to P.M. when the Muslim Women Protection Act, 1986 has been passed.

Respected Prime Minister

I recall my meeting with you a few days ago on the question of Muslim woman's protection bill. I gathered the impression that you hold the view that it would be open to any digent divorce to avail herself of the remedies under section 125 of the Cr.P.C. and alternatively under the new bill, the option being left to her. I thought it went a long way, although not wholly, to allay the fears of women. *The Times of India* carries a news item that the bill may be amended to mean that section 125 of Cr.P.C. will be available. If both parties, namely the divorce and divorcer, consent. This sabotage or frustrate the original view you mentioned. No husband in his senses will agree he be sued under the code when he can avoid the liability by refusing consent. The option must be left to the aggrieved party, namely the Muslim

43. V.R. Krishna Iyer, Human Rights and the Law, (1984), p. 32.
44. P. Krishna Swamy, Justice V.R. Krishna Iyer : A Living Legend, (2004), p. 227.
45. *Ibid.*
46. *Ibid.*

women. I hope the news report is wrong and in the impression. I gained about your intention is right. If the husband has to agree before the jurisdiction under the code scan be invoked, it makes an ass of the provision and only fools the people. I had been hoping—and do still hope—that the tumult which is tearing up the nation on this view Bill can be contained in the larger measure of the amendment is designed to give the women the option. May I request you one again to adopt what I consider is the only straight-forward course, short of withdrawals of the bill.[47]

With kindest regard

Yours sincerely

V.R. Krishna Iyer

He is also in favour of the common civil code and wanted amendment in the Bill and wanted the implementation of Cr.P.C. 125 on Muslim and Hindu Women.

But Karlminger put it as, "the voice of the intelligence is soft and weak said Frued. It is drowned out by roar of tear. It is ignored by the voice of desire. It is contradicted by voice of same. It is hissed away by hate and extinguished by anger. Most of all it is silenced by ignorance.

In the Act Justice Iyer wanted to give the option to the women, therefore, he wrote a letter for Prime Minister and Speaker of Lok Sabha. But Bill has been passed and remains condition as before the judgment of Shah Bano case.[48] But by this Act one thing is clear, religion is above the law. But Justice Iyer in his book 'Law and Religion' has said that man has made the religion, religion has not made the man. We cannot ignore the legal jurisprudence on the basis of religion. Justice Iyer said law is based on experience but no logic but Cardzo say where the experience silent then law is functionary. Justice Iyer says that it is long struggle which has to fight for women emancipation therefore he quoted line of Churchill, "This is

47. V.R. Krishna Iyer, The Muslim Women Protection Act, 1986 (1987), p. 101.
48. *Ibid.*, p. 100.

not to be end, it is not even the beginning of the end. But it is perhaps, the end of beginning." Our Constitution or other legal laws demands gender justice.

4.7 SUM UP

Justice V.R. Krishna Iyer is the living legend of Indian judicial system. He is every inch gentleman. He gave some dynamic judgments on various issues like industrial jurisprudence, prison system, death penalty, distributive justice and gender justice. He had delivered about 400 judgments which are masterpiece in itself. The lines of Sain Fruncis of Asis have appropriately implemented on Justice V.R. Krishna Iyer.

> Lord makes me on instrument of your peace
> Where there is hatred, let me sow love
> Where there is injury, pardon
> Where there is despair, hope
> Where is darkness, light
> And where there is sadness, joy

Justice V.R. Krishna Iyer is true struggler for justice. His legal Darwinism is different from the other legal doyen and experts of law. As student, lawyer, minister, humanist and cultivate involved in a hundred cause he remembered and often quoted Goethe's great lines, "who never ate bread in sorrow, who never spent the darksome hours weeping and waiting for morrow, he know ye not, ye heavenly powers.[49]

He is modest and most cultivated man in legal field. From beginning as Justice in 1973 he has faced the agitation from 150 Advocates who boycotted the court of Justice V.R. Krishna Iyer, but Iyer never had feeling of ill-will towards those Advocates. Soji Sobrajee accepted as mistake when V.R. Krishna Iyer retired from the Supreme Court of India. He always said that a man is not judged by big treats but by those values which he has adopted and aloft high.

49. P. Krishnaswamy, Justice V.R. Krishna Iyer—A Living Legend, (2004), p. 4.

The decision of Justice V.R. Krishna Iyer in a case of *Indira Nehru Gandhi* v. *Raj Narain,*[50] was not merely milestone but national event from any point of view. This case has established Justice V.R. Krishna Iyer as impartial Judge. I want to quote lines of Kipling's poem in a good lesson for judge too.

> "If you can talk with crowds and keep your virtue
> or walk both with king—nor lose the common touch
> If nether foes or loving friends can hurt you
> It all man court with you none to much
> With sixty seconds' worth of distance run
> Yours' earth and everything that's in it
> And which is more—you will be man my son.[51]

Justice V.R. Krishna Iyer is strong supporter of social justice. He is single man army. He always said that we have no other earth why we fight each other. He always took voice against injustice to common man. In his book 'Judge Portpouri' quoted these lines:

> First they come for the Jews and
> I did not speak out because I was not Jew
> Then they come for the communists
> And I did not speak out—because I was not communist
> Then they come for the trade unionist
> And I did not speak out because I was trade unionist
> Then they came for me
> And there was no one left to speak out for me.

No we must speak out last we should be lost in mute mortality. We are not slaves.[52]

These lines will reveal character conduct of Justice V.R. Krishna Iyer. He is every inch gentleman. He supported industrial jurisprudence and common man's right. It can be said that Justice V.R. Krishna Iyer is bold man for common

---

50. AIR 1975 SC 2299.
51. P. Krishnaswamy, Justice V.R. Krishna Iyer—A Living Legend, (2004), p. 132.
52. V.R. Krishna Iyer, Judge Postpouri, (2007), p. 38.

man's right. He is simple but his functions extraordinary. He came under the definition of progressive Judge. He believed that Judge can speak throughout his judgment. These lines can be very suitable for Justice V.R. Krishna Iyer.

A rose does need to preach
It simply spreads its fragrance
Fragrance is its non-sermon

Iyer is man of conventional sense. His concept of social justice has been supported by various sections of people. Perhaps Justice V.R. Krishna Iyer is single man in history of Supreme Court whose judgments never repealed till today. He has been charged for contempt of court twice. But Justice Iyer said that nobody is above social justice and common man cause. Judiciary is under the Constitution not over the Constitution. There is lakshman rekha which is known as Constitution. Every body is under Constitution not above the Constitution. Constitution is a human document. Therefore, in *Sunil Batra case* said that prisoner should have the constitutional rights. But in last we can say that the philosophers have only interpreted the world in various ways, the point is to change it.

5

Conclusion

The concept of social justice embodies a dynamic, modern idea. It is a modern idea because the ancient and medieval societies generally accepted the differences in status and opportunities open to different sections of society as sacrosanct; but with the dawn of modern age these differences were subjected to close scrutiny as to whether they were based on rational grounds or not. It is a dynamic idea because its demands are not fixed.

Social justice, a multi dimensional concept, has been viewed by scholars of political science, philosophy and law. Like wise school of individual thinker considers natural rights as the touchstone of justice or injustice for proprietarian theory of justice. The essence of justice is that charter is just and maintains the standards of right and wrong,[1] proper and improper and that government should respect basic civil and political liberties; the utilitarian philosopher seek justice in the principle of "greatest good of greatest number."

The founding father of Indian Constitution adopted a holistic view of social justice and enshrined its basic principle

1. B.R. Purhoit, Sandeep Joshi, "Social Justice in India", (2003), p. 11.

in the preamble of the Constitution is also starts with the words be the people of India and provide the socio-economic and political justice.

Social justice is infact conscience of Indian Constitution, because Indian Constitution is committed to reconstructing Indian society characterized not only by the ideals of liberty, equality and fraternity but also justice: social, economic and political.

When Indian got freedom, at that time there were so many disparities in the sphere of social, economic and political fields. But our founding fathers of Indian Constitution enrolled the three great words in the Preamble that social, economic and political justice. Social justice requires equality and liberty to all, irrespective of education, caste, creed, race, religion, status and sex. Economic justice requires no discrimination between two persons on the basic of economic values. As a matter of fact, economic justice is a corollary of social justice as it necessarily demands a socialistic pattern of society. Nehru told the constituent assembly that its first task was "to free Indian through a new constitution to every Indian fullest opportunity to his capacity. He believes that new constitution itself will lead to the real freedom which would bring all manner of opportunities or progress to the Indian masses".[2]

The Indian Constitution has deep aspiration of Constitution makers regarding social economic and political justice. It is instrument of social engineering and social development. It is not a paper work or mere document; it has contained human values, human emotions and feelings. If you denies the person from Constitution it means you denied the person from humanity. Our Constitution has also discussed the fundamental rights and directive principles of state policy, these two are vehicle of social justice.

Constitution also puts the limitations on other organs of the government for example, legislative, executive and judiciary. Parliament is making the law and executive set it in motion and judiciary interpreted the law. Judiciary interpreted the law according to people need and common man problems.

2. *Ibid.*, p. 25.

But when we talk about the function of judiciary, then we have to made concentration on the rule of judges. Judges interpreted the Constitution according to needs of the society. "The purpose of the law, and the purpose of the judiciary, is not merely to sit in wig and gown for a number of hours a day on look every learned. They supply a social purpose that is bring about justice, to deliver justice to the people".[3]

The concept of social justice has deep historical roots, it starts with human civilization, "if we see history of social justice, it is very deep. From Plato to Hegal to Marx and Marx to John Rawls talks about social justice".

Benthem also support that main function of the government was to promote happiness of the society by furthering the enjoyment of pleasure, and affording security against pain. Benthem concept of social justice is based on the theory of Greatest good of Greatest number.[4]

On the other hand Marxian's social justice is based on the distribution of means of production in the favour of common man.

In Hindu Jurisprudence is based on the concept of Dharma, and Dharma is also based on just and good society. In Manusmriti it has been said that King has to follow the Dharma. In Arthsasthra Kautilayan also gave the stress on state's functioning in common man favour and their upliftment. The concept of social justice has been deeply rooted in Mahabharata and Ramayana. Gita has also given the philosophy of Dharma, and give the message one should has to fight for the protection of Dharma. That is why it can be said that concept of social justice as old as human civilization. Our culture heritage also elaborates the concept of social justice in a very progressive and dynamic way. Even if we see the freedom struggle it also based on social economic and political justice. After the independence government has adopted the various policies for providing the social justice. That's why Indian planning system was based on social, political and economic justice, various land reforms has been occurred for providing social justice. Many economic

3. *Ibid.*
4. Jullious Stone, Human Law and Human Justice, (2000), p. 125.

programmes such as IRDP, NREP, DPAP and FWP are based on social justice. It can be said that social justice has remained in the society from the very beginning of human civilization, but its forms has been changed with human civilization. But human being has deep urge for social justice, that's why no body can denies the social justice to the common man. Therefore, our Constitution is a social document which based on social, economic and political justice.

His main object of life to provide social justice to the common man, down trodden human beings. He always stands for common cause of human beings. His contribution in Indian Constitution is not small one. He has given marvelous interpretation on Fundamental Rights and Directive Principles. He always said that Directive Principlc is based on the concept of social justice. He always stress for implementation of Directive Principles and said that Directive Principles deals with the weaker section of society and Fundamental Rights deals with upper section of the society. If you want to provide social justice to the society you have to make balance between social good or individual good.

The judge's mission he said is that of securing justice to every citizen in the country and creating a just society amidst us.

> "In India today judges have not merely to adjudicate on rights and wrongs, but have to be sentinels on the qui vive. They face never challenge; shoulder a vast range of responsibility in upholding the constitution and the laws. The social goals enshrined in the Preamble to our Constitution, the fundamental rights chapter and the Directive Principles of State Policy broadly and vaguely project our current policy philosophy. The judicial organ, being part of the State, shares and the national objective and perspective of political and economic democracy and spells out from the article of the Constitution and corpus juri's of India legal framework of a secular society with egalitarian urges, thus deporting from the old order and conservative common law concept.[5]

5. M.P.R. Nair, "Justice V.R. Krishna Iyer at 90", Ed., 2005, p. 85.

According to Iyer our Constitution starts with the people of India and it also provide the social economic and political justice that's why Justice V.R. Krishna Iyer said that:

> "Social justice is the signature tune of our Constitution and the little man in peril of losing his liberty is the consumer of social justice. A nobler sentiment than this is hard to find."[6]

But for providing the social justice to citizen there is need for synthesis of fundamental right and directive principle of state policy.

That is why Justice Iyer said that in the process of interpretation, Part IV of the Constitution must enter the soul of Part III and the laws. Humanism and compassion are fundamental duties which are non-negotiable since Part IV A articulate it with authority. To wipe every tear from every eye was favourite dream of our Constitution maker. But Justice V.R. Krishna Iyer is against new economic policy because it against the social justice. Because some corporate has arrived in India with hunger for profits. Iyer is of opinion that new economic policy is against Parts III, IV, IVA of Indian Constitution. Iyer said that our finance minister whichever, party in power, have gone for GATT, TRIPS, WTO which are loyal to American incorporated on the other hand Indian Constitution made promise for socialistic pattern of society. Justice Iyer concept of social justice is not exact, static or absolute concept. It is rather flexible, dynamic and relative one. All basic requirement of man,[7] material, cultural, and spiritual must be fulfilled. He sees the creative aspect of social justice in the opportunity to unfold each person's human potential-aesthetic intellectual, technical, physical or other. His concept of social justice can be summed up in the following words:

> Social justice is a generous concept which Assures to every member of society a fair deal, any remedial injury,

6. *Ibid.*, p. 85.
7. Shilja Chander, "Justice V.R. Krishna Iyer on Fundamental Rights and Directive Principles", Ed., 1998, p. 287.

injustice, inadequacy of disability falls within the liberal connotation of social injustice.[8]

Justice Iyer said that social justice as basis of progressive stability in society and human progress. Iyer of the opinion that the preamble of the Constitution, a basic postulate of the nation's founding faith expressly articulates the vision of nation as a social justice state with a dynamic, democratic, egalitarian order indeed, Parts III and IV are plainly Fabian socialist.

Role of judges in the interpretation of Indian Constitution is remarkable. Statutes are Skelton, only judiciary fill mass and blood in the statutes. That is why Frankfurter : remarks

> "A judge should be compounded of the faculties that are demanded of the historian and the philosopher and the prophet. The last demand upon him to make some forecast of the consequences of his action is perhaps the heaviest. To pierce the curtain of the future, to give shape and visage to mysteries till in the womb of time, is the gift of the imagination. It requires poetic sensibilities with which judges are rarely endowed and which their education does not normally develop. These judges must have something of the creative artist in them; they must have antennae registering feelings and judgment beyond logical, let alone quantitative proof".

As Earl Warren expressed:

> "Our judges are not monks or scientists, but participants in the living stream of our national life, steering the law between the dangers of rigidity on the one hand and of formlessness on the other. Our systems face no theoretical dilemma but a single continuous problem : how to apply to ever-changing conditions the never changing principles of freedom."[9]

8. *Ibid.*, p. 288.
9. Justice V.R. Krishna Iyer, "Legally Speaking", 2004, p. 146.

The Indian judges must rise to burning justice needs of our age. They can, given the training and technological and business management course plus discipline and ethics excel the best in any other country.[10] Many judges of Indian Supreme have given the big contribution to the development of concept of social justice. Justice V.R. Krishna Iyer is one of them. He is champion of social justice. According to him Indian constitution is deal with common man problem. Constitution is not a mere paper work, it is living organism and deeply related with human problem, human needs. That is why it can be said that role of Justice V.R. Krishna Iyer in Indian judiciary is not small one. He never missed such type of opportunity, where social justice is in question. Justice Iyer said that Indian Constitution is totally human document, therefore many legal persons express that.

For Justice V.R. Krishna Iyer :

> Law is a business to which my life is devoted, and I should show less than devotion if I did not to what in me lies to improve it, and when I perceive what seems to the ideal of the future, if I hesitated to point it out and to press towards it will all my heart.[11]

Justice Iyer said that after the 60 years of independence of Indian justice system still remain untouchable and non-approachable to the vast have-not humanity of the country. This is true at the level of the trial court, the appellate court, and the superior tribunals with binding finality and constitutional supremacy.[12] The performance of this great constitutional instrumentality is in need of a transformation. But the courts, when it suits them suffer, from amnesia of established maxims of trial justicia. Lethargy in court and indolence in disposal re-chronic forensic evils. It is good to remember the great judge Felix Frankfurter who said, "Judges as persons, or courts as institutions, are entitled to no greater

10. *Ibid.*, p. 172.
11. *Ibid.*
12. Justice V.R. Krishna Iyer, "Some Inconvenient Truth", *The Hindu*, Friday, December 14, 2007.

immunity from criticism than other persons or institutions. Just because the holders of judicial office are identified with the interest of justice they may forget their common human fragilities and fallibilities. As eminent U.S. Judge, Hugo Black observed, wisely and truly, what realism tells us daily "Judges are not essentially different from other government official".[13]

Fortunately they remain human even after assuming their judicial duties. Like all the rest of mankind they may be affected from time to time by pride and passion, by pettiness and bruised feeling, by improper understanding or by excessive zeal.[14]

According to Justice V.R. Krishna Iyer Judges must have pro-humanism approach regarding human problem. That is why justice Iyer said that, humanity, not legality, is social justice . . . social justice is a humanistic approach towards his fellow. It is based on the egalitarian society where everybody gets according to his needs and ability. Because centre point of every system is human development. Justice Iyer is strong supporter of human cause. He never missed the opportunity to write where the human cause in question in present days. He wrote letter to Parkash Karat and Governor of West Bengal[15] on the issue of Nandigram and criticizes the government method to settle the issue. Iyer wrote that you cannot deny humanity on basis of development. Development cannot be measured by things, it deals with human development. He said these things are against our constitutional jurisprudence as well as against human jurisprudence. You cannot be denied the human beings from the social justice, by pursuing west intoxicated civilization, where the money is everything. Iyer said that he cannot go above the humanity and human feelings. One has to maintain each and everything according to our constitutional philosophy,· because social, economic and political justices are our aim. We cannot ignore them on the basis of capitalistic jurisprudence. Directive Principles and fundamental rights are given in our Constitution. We must try implement to these principles only then we can expect the social justice. You cannot deny these two pillars, which has

13. *Ibid.*
14. *Ibid.*

great place in our Constitution. It can be said that justice Iyer has three things in his mind; the common man, Constitution, and social justice while he delivers the judgment: In real sense he is geeat jurist of India. He is man who can easily understand the human being. He is also proved this thing by this judgments during his term in Supreme Court of India. His every effort deals with human problems. He is every inch gentleman in his service. Humanity is aim of his judgments. Justice V.R. Krishna Iyer has given various judgments where social justice has been defined, such as the *Statesman Ltd.* v. *their Workman,* AIR 1976 SC 758, *Rohtas Industrial* v. *Its Union,* AIR 1976 SC 425, *Straw Board Mfg. Co.* v. *Its Workman,* AIR 1977 SC 741.

State of Kerala v. *N.M. Thomas,* AIR 1976 SC 940, *Nandani Sathpathy* v. *P.L. Dhani,* 1978 (2) SCC 424, *Sunil Batra* v. *Delhi Administration,* AIR 1977 SC 1926. All these above noted judgments are the landmark in the History of Supreme Court, which is given by Justice V.R. Krishna Iyer.

Justice V.R. Krishna Iyer has not lived in vain. He always make the efforts in the favour of common man. His social or humanistic approach towards society makes him popular in the Legal History of Indian apex Court. His mission of life can be summed up in the moving poem by Emily Dickinson:

> If I can stop one heart from breaking
> I shall not live in vain
> If I can ease one life the aching or, cool one pain
> Or help on fainting robin unto its next again
> I shall not live in vain,

Today he is 92 years, spent not in hankering after fame and fortune but in the service of humanity's not with pump and glory, but with transparent sincerity and true humility. That event is indeed on occasion for celebration and for paying tribute to this man for all reasons who has planted indelible foot prints on the sands of time.[16]

---

15. *Ibid.*
16. M.P.R. Nair, "Justice Krishna Iyer at 90", Ed., 2005, p. 54.

Iyer's contribution in Indian Constitution cannot be discussed within few words. In his various judgments he says that the Indian Constitution is a great social document, almost revolutionary in its aim of transforming a medieval, hierarchical society into modern egalitarian democracy. In *state of Kerala* v. *N.M. Thomas* in a separate opinion justice Iyer said that:

> Re-distributive justice to Harijan humanity insist on effective reforms designed to produce equal partnership of the erstwhile "lowliest and the lost" by state action informed by short-run and long-run sociologically potent perspective planning and implementation. An uneven socio-economic landscape hardly gives the joy of equal opportunity and development or draws forth their best form of manpower reserves now following in the law visibility areas of discontent life.[17]

He also gave big contribution in the development of industrial jurisprudence in the Bangalore *Water Supply case, the Statesman Ltd.* v. *their Workman, Mumbai Kamgar Sabha, Rohtas Industries, Straw Board Mfg*. In these cases Justice Iyer widen the dimension of industrial justice with help of concept of social justice. In *Sunil Batra case* Justice Iyer observed that social justice cannot sleep if the Constitution hang limp where its consumer most need its humanism for him social justice in the prison context has a functional veracity hardly explored. The roots of our Constitution lie deep in the finer spiritual source of social justice, beyond the melting point of bad politicking feudal crudities and sublimated sadism sustaining itself by profound faith in man and his latent divinity and the confidence that you can accomplish by kindness what you cannot do by force.[18]

His contribution in Indian Constitution is marvelous. In other words, it can be said that Justice V.R. Krishna Iyer is the living legend of Indian Judicial system. He is every inch gentleman. He has given various judgments on industrial

17. K.D. Gour, "Criminal Law and Criminology", Ed., 2002, p. 516.
18. AIR 1978 SC 1675.

jurisprudence prison system, death penalty, distributive justice and gender justice. But by these judgments he always ready to provide social justice. Social Justice is the base while he delivering judgment. His humanistic approach towards every living being is incredible. He has the deep compassion towards human suffering and human feelings. These lines are most appropriate on Justice V.R. Krishna Iyer.

> Lord make me an instrument of your peace
> "Where there is hatred, let me sow love
> Where there is injury, pardon
> Where there is despair, hope
> Where there is darkness, light
> And where there is sadness joy"[19]
> Saint Francis of Assisi

Iyer never miss the opportunity where the human cause in question. He has common touch to all human beings that is why lines of Kipling poem is most suit on justice Krishna Iyer:

> If you can talk with crowds and keep your virtue
> Or walk with King—nor lose the common touch
> It neither foes or loving friend can hurt you
> If all men count with you none to much
> With sixty seconds, worth of distance run
> Your's earth and everything that is in it
> And which is more—you will be man my son[20]

Justice Iyer in real sense is a great intellectual of Indian judicial system. In the end I want to say one thing that my work is small in before of this legal doyen, compassionate human being a true social worker moreover a human judge.

Life for justice Iyer is verb not a noun. It is perennial process not final product. Justice Krishna Iyer philosophy and basic value set are best expressed in his own words.

---

19. P. Krishna Swamy, "Justice V.R. Krishna Iyer—A Living Legend", Ed., 2004, p. 4.
20. *Ibid.*, p. 132.

I hold deep in my soul that I am a Human and so anything that distress any living creatures deeply disturbs me and commands me into curative action, even if in vain. I am aware of my weaknesses and I feel painfully inefficient when injustice is inflicted on fellow creatures.

As a judge, he administrated law with human kindness and compassion, justice with mercy and karuna as an activists judge open new vistas of judicial activism in most branches of law and fearlessly but successfully challenged out moded laws and changed the course, content and context of judicial system. He is a man of passion committed to the down trodden and toiling masses. He extended juristic principles to the utmost in the service of the people. According to him Constitution of India represents the people's vision of India to be and is meant, not for richest of the rich but for poorest of the poor.[21] That is why Mr. R.J. Kocher of progressive law association:

> "Indian jurisprudence today is not what it would have been had justice Krishna Iyer never existed".[22]

He has given big contribution for the development of constitutional jurisprudence, criminal jurisprudence or industrial jurisprudence with human jurisprudence. Life has many roles but some person play their role in such way which inspire the future generation. Justice Krishna Iyer is complete institution that is why he always quoted the lines of Lord R.B. Haldone:

> What ultimately matter in one's life is not the result or the success or failure but the quality of the work, the passion that is brought to bear upon anything that one takes in his mind.[23]

For him life is not measure by success but by those values which the man Adolph high. He is every inch gentleman. He

21. M.P.R. Nair, "Justice Krishna Iyer at 90", Ed., 2005, p. 88.
22. *Ibid.*, p. 92.
23. *Ibid.*, p. 138.

is true philosopher of Indian society. That is why justice P.N. Bhagwati said:

> That "Justice V.R. Krishna Iyer is not only a great judge, not only profound legal school, not only a bold innovator, not only a powerful spokesman for social justice but also close and intimate friend.

Justice V.R. Krishna Iyer has no live in vain today, he is 95 years spent not in hankering, after time and fortune but in service of humanity's not with pump and glory, but with transparent sincerity and true humility. He is men for all seasons. He helped to humanize the legal system particularly in the field of criminal jurisprudence and jail reform. He made no secret of the fact that judge must have a social philosophy and humane approach to legal protection. Whilst Subhu Rao has obsessive concern with fundamental right, Krishna Iyer concern was broader for poor and downtrodden. He curved out a special entrance for destitute in the somewhat formidable portal of Supreme Court.[24]

His social philosophy was more than an interpretive tool. It has been the mainspring of almost all his judicial dicta. He founded this new school of jurisprudence which has many adherents. It still has Law of any given society is the expression of the push of social force in that society and we cannot explain its substance or its operation without regard to those forces. That is why, in the last forty years, there has been a growing movement towards a less formal, and more realistic, jurisprudence. The relation between sociology and law has grown even more intimate, and a jurisprudence of normal couples now satisfies few save the veterans of an earlier age. Law is regarded as binding because, it is useful, or because it embodies reason or because it is a search for those canons of behaviour the observance of which will maximize the satisfaction of demand.[25] Law ultimately, therefore is body of rules which seek to fulfil the object of the state.[26]

24. *Ibid.*, p. 57.
25. Harold Laski, A Grammer of Politics, Anamika Publishers, p. 21.
26. *Op. cit.*, p. 22.

Table of Cases

E. Annumma *v.* State of A.P., AIR 1974 SC 799, 98
The Statesman Ltd. *v.* Their Workmen, AIR 1976 SC 758, 72
Mumbai Kamghar Sabha *v.* Abdul Bhai AIR 1976 SC 1455, 29, 72
Rohtas Industries *v.* Its Union, AIR 1976 SC 425, 73
Straw Board Mfg. *v.* Its Workmen, AIR 1977 SC 941, 73
Bangalore Water Supply *v.* A. Rajappa, AIR 1978 SC 548, 74
B. Benerjee *v.* Anita, AIR 1975 SC 1146, 74
Jolly George Varghees *v.* Bank of Cochin, AIR 1980 SC 470, 105
Moti Ram *v.* State of M.P., AIR 1978 SC 1595, 104
Prem Shankar Shukla *v.* Delhi Administration, AIR 1980 SC 1535, 105
Mohammed Giasudin *v.* State of A.P., AIR 1977 SC 1926, 110
Shiv Mohan Singh *v.* State of Delhi, AIR 1977 SC 949, 110
N.K. Chauhan *v.* State of Gujarat, AIR 1977 SC 251, 106
State of Kerala *v.* N.M. Thomas, AIR 1976 SC 490, 77, 106
ABSK Sangh *v.* Union of India, AIR 1981 SC 298, 106
Charles Sobraj *v.* Supdt. Central Jail, Tihar, AIR 1978 SC 1514, 108
M.H. Hoskot *v.* State of Maharashtra, AIR 1978 SC 1548, 109
P.N. Kaushal *v.* UOI, AIR 1978 SC 1457, 109
Bar Council *v.* M.V. Dabholkar, AIR 1976 SC 242, 109
Maneka Gandhi *v.* Union of India, AIR 1978 SC 597.
Sunil Batra *v.* Delhi Administration, AIR 1978 SC 1675, 103, 126

Golak Nath *v.* State of Punjab, AIR 1967 SC 1643, 87
Kesavanand Bharti *v.* State of Kerala, AIR 1973 SC 1461, 87
Minerva Mills Ltd. *v.* Union of India, AIR 1980 SC 1789, 88
Indira Nehru Gandhi *v.* Raj Narain, AIR 1975 SC 2299, 116
Jalubhai Nanabhai Kachar *v.* State of Gujarat, AIR 1995 SC 142, 89
Markendya *v.* State of A.P., AIR 1989 SC 1308, 90
Hanif Qurashi Mohd. *v.* State of Bihar, AIR 1958 SC 731, 93

Bibliography

Books

A.N. Sen, "Human Right", Sri Sai Law Publications, First Ed., 2002.

Ashok S. Chousalkar, "Social and Political Implication of Concept of Justice and Dharma", Mittal Publishing, 1986.

B. Shiva Rao, "The Framing of Indian Constitution", N.M. Tripathi Pivate Ltd., Ed., 1968.

B.R. Sharma, "Socio-Economic Justice under Indian Constitution", New Delhi, Deep & Deep, Ed., 1984.

Benjamin N. Cardozo, "The Nature of the Judicial Process", Universal Law Publishing House, 1987.

Chandrika Singh, "Constitutional Battle in Indian for Socio-Economic Justice", First Ed., 2001.

Chaturvedi, "Justice Natural Social Political & Economic", The Law Book Company, Ed., 1990.

Huntington Crain's, "Legal Philosophy from Plato to Hegal", Ed., 1966.

D.D. Basu, "Shorter Constitutional Law of India", Wadhwa Law and Company Nagpur, Rep., 2003.

Dr. S.H. Patil, "Gandhi and Swaraj", Deep & Deep, 1983.

Harihar Prasad Dubey, "The Judicial System of India", 1968.

Edgar Bodenheimer, "Jurisprudence Revised Edition, the Philosophy and Method of the Law", Universal Law Publishers Ltd., 2001.

J.S. Verma, "New Dimension of Justice", Universal Law Publishing Co., Pvt. Ltd., 2000.

Justice Swarup, "For Whom the Law is Made", Veena Publishers, Ed., 1981.

Justice V.R. Krishna Iyer, "A Constitutional Miscellany", Lucknow Eastern Book, 1986.

Justice V.R. Krishna Iyer, "Dr. Ambedkar and the Dalit Future, Delhi, B.R. Publishing, 1990.

Justice V.R. Krishna Iyer, "Equal Justice and Forensic Process: Truth and Myth", Lucknow Eastern Book, (1986).

Justice V.R. Krishna Iyer, "Freedom of Information", Lucknow Eastern Book, 1990.

Justice V.R. Krishna Iyer, "Human Right Judge Miscellany", B.R. Publishing Corporation, 1995.

Justice V.R. Krishna Iyer, "Human Rights and Inhuman Wrong", Delhi B.R. Publishing,1990.

Justice V.R. Krishna Iyer, "Human Rights and the Law", Indore, Ved Pal, 1984.

Justice V.R. Krishna Iyer, "Indian Justice Perspective and Problem", Indore, Ved Pal Law, 1984.

Justice V.R. Krishna Iyer, "Indian Social Justice in Crisis", Madras Affiliated East-West Ed., 1983.

Justice V.R. Krishna Iyer, "Judge Postpouri", Universal Law Publishing, Ed., 2007.

Justice V.R. Krishna Iyer, "Judicial Justice : A New Focus Towards Social Justice".

Justice V.R. Krishna Iyer, "Justice and Beyond", New Delhi, Deep & Deep Publications, 1980.

Justice V.R. Krishna Iyer, "Law and Life", Vikas Publishing, 1979.

Justice V.R. Krishna Iyer, "Law and Religion", Deep & Deep Publications, Ed., 1984.

Justice V.R. Krishna Iyer, "Law, Lawyer and Justice, Delhi, B.R. Publishing, 1989.

Justice V.R. Krishna Iyer, "Law Versus Justice : Problem and Solution", New Delhi, Deep & Deep Publishers, 1981.

Justice V.R. Krishna Iyer, "Legally Speaking", Delhi Universal Law Publishing, Ed., 2004.

Justice V.R. Krishna Iyer, "Minorities Civil Liberties and Criminal Justice", New Delhi, People Publishing House, 1980.

Justice V.R. Krishna Iyer, "Our Courts on Trial", B.R. Publishing, 1987.

Justice V.R. Krishna Iyer, "Perspective in Criminology Law and Social Change", New Delhi, Allied Publishers, 1980.

Justice V.R. Krishna Iyer, "Salvaging Democracy, Some Reflections", Delhi, Konark, 1990.

Justice V.R. Krishna Iyer, "Social Justice, Sunset or Dawn, 2nd Ed., Lucknow, Eastern Book, 1987.

Justice V.R. Krishna Iyer, "Social Mission of Law", Orient Longman Ltd., 1976.

Justice V.R. Krishna Iyer, "Some Left Hidden Aspect of Indian Social Justice", Lucknow, Eastern Book, 1980.

Justice V.R. Krishna Iyer, "The Indian Presidency's Nascent Challenges and Novel Responses", New Delhi, Deep & Deep Publishers Pvt. Ltd., 1988.

Justice V.R. Krishna Iyer, "The Muslim Women Protection of Right on Divorce Act, 1986", Lucknow, Eastern Bank, 1987.

Justice V.R. Krishna Iyer, "The Social Dimension of Law and Justice in Contemporary India, The Dynamics of New Jurisprudence: Problem and Prospects", Nagpur, All India Reporter, 1979.

Justice V.R. Krishna Iyer, Law, Justice and the Disabled, New Delhi, Deep & Deep Publishing, 1982.

M. Rama Jois, "Legal and Constitutional History of India", N.M. Tripathi Publishing Ltd., 1990.

M.C. Kagzi, "The Constitution of India", India Law House, Ed., 2004.

M.C. Markandan, "Directive Principle of State Policy in the Indian Constitution", A.B.S. Publications, Ed., 1989.

M.P.R. Nair, "Justice Krishna Iyer at 90", Universal Law Publishing, Ed., 2005.

M.V. Pylee, Constitutional Law of India", Bar Council Trusts, Ed., 1984.

Murphy, "Law and Poverty", N.M. Tripathi Private Ltd., Ed. 1973.

O.P. Gauba, "Dimension of Social Justice", Ed., 1983.
Prof. K.C. Gopal Krishna, "Legal Economics, International Dimension of Economics and Law", Eastern Book Company, Ed., 1998.
Quil Ahmad, "Mohamdan Law", Central Law Agency, Ed., 2000.
Rama Jois, "Ancient Indian Law", Universal Law Publishing, 2004.
Rama Jois, "Seeds of Modern Public Law in Ancient Indian Jurisprudence", Eastern Book Company, 2000.
S.M.N. Raina, "Law, Judges and Justice", Dialogue Publications, New Delhi, Ed., 1986.
S.N. Johari, "Industrial Jurisprudence, Ed., 1984.
Sherful Hasan, "Supreme Court : Fundamental Rights and Directive Principle", Deep & Deep Publications, Ed., 1981.
Shilja Chander, "Justice V.R. Krishna Iyer on Fundamental Rights and Directive Principles, Deep & Deep Publishing, 1998.
Sudesh Kumar Sharma, "Directive Principle and Fundamental Right, New Delhi, Deep & Deep, 1990.
Sudesh Kumar Sharma, "Distributive Justice under Indian Constitution with Reference to Right to Equality and Property", New Delhi, Deep & Deep, 1989.
U.C. Sarkar, Epoch of Hindu Legal History, Ed., 1958.
V.K. Gupta, "Kautilyan Jurisprudence", B.D. Gupta Publishing, Ed., 1987.
V.N. Shukla, "Constitution of India", Lucknow, Eastern Publishers Ed., 2006.
William Ebenstin, "Great Political Thinker", Oxford IBH Publishing Co., 1975.

Editorials in Newspapers

Justice V.R. Krishna Iyer, An Open Letter to West Bengal Governor, *The Hindu*, Saturday, Nov., 3, 2007.
Justice V.R. Krishna Iyer, "Democracy and the Election Process", *The Hindu*, Wednesday 4, 2007.
Justice V.R. Krishna Iyer, "Executive Cannot Act Independently of Parliament on Nuclear Deal", *The Hindu*, Thursday, Sept. 13, 2007.

Justice V.R. Krishna Iyer, Judicial Reform in the Indian Context, *The Hindu*, Saturday, May 12, 2007.

Justice V.R. Krishna Iyer, Unifying Personal Law, *The Hindu*, Saturday, Sept., 6, 2003.

Justice V.R. Krishna Iyer, The Dynamics of Access to Justice, *The Hindu*, Tuesday, May 29, 2007.

Justice V.R. Krishna Iyer, National Judicial Commission, *The Hindu*, Monday, October 20, 2003.

Justice V.R. Krishna Iyer, "There was no Hidden Agenda", Mr. Nariman, *The Hindu*, Tuesday, June 28, 2005.

Justice V.R. Krishna Iyer, "Ban on Strikes : A Judicial Excess"? *The Hindu*, Thursday, October 2, 2003.

Justice V.R. Krishna Iyer, "Rivers Sand and People's Survival, *The Hindu*, January 23, 2003.

Justice V.R. Krishna Iyer, "House Privileges and the Courts, *The Hindu*, Thursday, November 27, 2003.

Journal

A.K. Koul, "Developing Countries in the GATT/WTO : Their Obligations and the Law", *Indian Journal of International Law*, Vol. 44, 2004.

B.L. Nirmal, "Poverty and Human Right : An Indian Context, Vol. 46, *Indian Journal of International Law*, 2006.

Emmanul Okon, "Land Law as an Instrument of Social Change", *JILI*, Vol. 31:2, p. 194 (1989).

G.S. Sharma, "Concept of Leadership Implicit in the Directive Principles of State Policy in the Indian Constitution, *JILI*, Vol. (7) (P) 173, 1965.

G.S. Sharma, "Economic Justice and the Indian Constitution : Some Implications of the Bonus Case", *JILI*, Vol. 8, 1966.

O.P. Parmer, ILO and India in Pursuit of Human Rights Through Labour Standards, Vol. 23 (P) 555 10, *JILI*, 1981.

Paramanand Singh, "Social Justice for Harijan : Some Legal Problems of Identification", Conversion and Judicial Review, Vol. 20:3, *JILI* 355, 1978.

Praveen Pavani, Indian Supreme Court and Worker-oriented Industrial Jurisprudence, *JILI*, Vol. 27:1, (1985).

Suresh C. Srivastava, "Labour Welfare and the Law", *JILI*, Vol. 17:3, 1975.

Wahab O. Egdewole, "Globalization and Its Challenges on National Legal System—A Case Study of Nigeria", Vol. 43, 2003.

Civil and Military Law Journals

Justice V.R. Krishna Iyer and Justice D.A. Desai, "The Deadly Quandary", *Civil and Military Law Journal*, Vol. 15, January-March, 1979.

Justice V.R. Krishna Iyer, "The Judicial System—Has It a Functional Future in Our Constitutional Order", Vol. 15, July-Sept., 1979.

Justice V.R. Krishna Iyer, "Beyond Human Justice", Vol. 16, Jan. to March, 1980.

Justice V.R. Krishna Iyer, "The Pathology of Indian Criminology and Its Prognosis", Vol. 12, January-March, 1976.

Justice V.R. Krishna Iyer, "Jurisprudence—A New Journey", Vol. 18, January-March, 1982.

Justice V.R. Krishna Iyer, "An Ideal Judge", Vol. 18, March-June, 1982.

Justice V.R. Krishna Iyer, "Three Decades of Constitutional Experience", Vol. 17, Jan.-March, 1981.

Justice V.R. Krishna Iyer, "Developmental Democracy Industrial-oriented Law", Vol. 17, October-November, 1981.

Justice V.R. Krishna Iyer, "Syndrome Ails Judiciary", Vol. 25, July-October, 1989.

Justice V.R. Krishna Iyer, "A Study of Indian Soviet Socialism", Vol. 19, Jan.-March, 1983.

Justice V.R. Krishna Iyer, "We the People of India", Vol. 19, April-June, 1983.

Justice V.R. Krishna Iyer, "Law, Justice and Litigation", Vol. 31, January-March, 1995.

Justice V.R. Krishna Iyer, "Our Founding Deed and Our Fighting Creed : Some Thoughts and Their Future", Vol. 20, January-March, 1984.

Justice V.R. Krishna Iyer, "Jurisprudence and Jurisprudence", Vol. 11, Oct.-Dec., 1975.

Justice V.R. Krishna Iyer, "The Suicide Syndrome", Vol. 32, June-March, 1996.

Justice V.R. Krishna Iyer, "The Judicial System, has it a Functional Future in Our Constitutional Order", Vol. 32, July-Sept., 1996.

Justice V.R. Krishna Iyer, "Social Justice, Romane and Reality : Social Justice Sun Down or Dim Down", Vol. 27, Jan.-March.

Justice V.R. Krishna Iyer, "Pendent and Information", Vol. 23, April-June, 1987.

Justice V.R. Krishna Iyer, "Crime and Correctional Processes, Key Issue in Contemporary Criminology", Vol. 28, Oct.-Dec., 1992.

Justice V.R. Krishna Iyer, "Old Law *versus* New Justice", Vol. 28, April-June, 192.

Justice V.R. Krishna Iyer, "The Parameters and Perils of Dissent by Direct Action", Vol. 28, July-Sept., 1992.

Justice V.R. Krishna Iyer, "A New Legal Order for Free India", Vol. 29, Oct.-Nov., 1993.

Justice V.R. Krishna Iyer, "Doctor Cannot Claim Immunity", Vol. 29, April-June, 1993.

Justice V.R. Krishna Iyer, "Processual Justice to the People : Some Institutional Perspective", Vol. 21, Jan.-March, 1985.

K.D. Gaur, "Criminal Law and Criminology", Deep and Publishers, 2002.

Index

Ancient Indian Thinkers and Concept of Social Justice,

British Era and Concept of Social Justice, 48

Classical Era and Concept of Social Justice:
Hugo Grotius, 32
Thomas Hobbes, 33
Locke, 33
Rousseau, 34
Benthem, 34
Classification of Justice, 66
Concept of Fundamental Rights, 53
Concept of Social Justice:
Historical Development, 25
Justice Iyer, 5
Constitution of Court, 43
Constitution of India and Concept of Social Justice, 53
Criminal Justice, 107

Daridra Narayana, 19
Dev, Guru Nanak, 42
Dimension of Social Justice, 63
Directive Principles and Social Justice, 80
Directive Principles of State Policy, 54
Distributive Justice, 76

Economic Justice, 66
Economic Reforms and Employment, 59
Economic Reform:
Impact on Poverty, 58
Economic Thinkers and Concept of Social Justice:
Pigou, 36
Equal Remuneration Act, 1976, 71

Factory Act, 1948, 71
Fundamental Rights and Directive Principles:
Relationship, 85

Gandhian Concept of Social Justice, 51
Gandhi, Indira, 79
Gandhi, Maneka, 59
Goswami Tulsidas, 42
Gender Justice, 111

Hindu Jurisprudence and the Concept of Social Justice, 37

Indian Constitutional Development, 48
Industrial Justice, 70
Islamic Approach to Social Justice, 45

Judicial Justice, 74
Judicial Postulates, 95
Judicial System and Concept of Social Justice, 43
  Punishment, 44
  Ordeal by Balance, 44
  Ordeal by Fire, 44
  Ordeal by Water, 44
  Ordeal by Poison, 44
  Ordeal by lot, 44
  Ordeal by Rice Grains, 44
  Ordeal by Fountain, 45
Justice V.R. Krishna Iyer:
  Brief Biography, 4
  Social Justice, 8
  View Regarding Constitution of India, 15
  His Language and Controversy, 14
  Concept of Law, 12
  Constitutional Justice, 77

Kabira, 41
Kautilya and Social Justice, 39

Land Reform, 56
Law and Justice, 99

Manusmriti and Concept of Social Justice, 38
Marxian View of Social Justice, 35
Maternity Benefit Act, 1961, 71
Minimum Wages Act, 1948, 71

Namboodripad, E.M.S., 4
New Economic Policy, 57

Organization of Village Self-Government, 84

Pandit Nehru's Vision of Social Justice, 50
Pascal, Blaise, 5
Payment of Bonus Act, 1965, 71
Payment of Gratuity Act, 1972, 71
Planning and Social Justice, 54
Political Justice, 69
Prison Justice, 103

Ramayana, Mahabharata and Concept of Social Justice, 40
Rao, P.V. Narasimha, 57
Religious Thinkers and Concept of Social Justice:
  Thomas Aquinas, 31
Reservation Policy, 105
Round Table Conference, 49
Rule of Law, 14

Saint Ravi Das, 43
Sapru, Tej Bahadur, 49
Servai, H.M., 14
Social and Economic Justice, 10
Social Justice:
  Concept, 2
  Dr. B.R. Ambedkar's View, 52
  Meaning, 26
  Ancient Western Thoughts, 29
    Plato, 29
    Aristotle, 30
    Cicero, 31
Sociological Thinkers and Social Justice:
  Roscoe Pound, 35

Trade Union Act, 1926, 71

Workmen Compensation Act, 1947, 71